DRUG EDUCATION LIBRARY

MARIJUANA

ABUSE AND LEGALIZATION

By Anna Collins

Portions of this book originally appeared in *Marijuana* by Hal Marcovitz

Published in 2017 by
Lucent Press, an Imprint of Greenhaven Publishing LLC
353 3rd Avenue
Suite 255
New York, NY 10010

Designer: Andrea Davison-Bartolotta
Editor: Jennifer Lombardo

Cataloging-in-Publication Data

Names: Collins, Anna.
Title: Marijuana: abuse and legalization / Anna Collins.
Description: New York : Lucent Press, 2017. | Series: Drug education library | Includes index.
Identifiers: ISBN 9781534560017 (library bound) | ISBN 9781534560024 (ebook)
Subjects: LCSH: Marijuana–Juvenile literature. | Marijuana–Therapeutic use–Juvenile literature. | Marijuana abuse–Juvenile literature.
Classification: LCC HV5822.M3 C65 2017 | DDC 362.29'5–dc23

Printed in the United States of America

CPSIA compliance information: Batch #CW17KL: For further information contact Greenhaven Publishing LLC, New York, New York at 1-844-317-7404.

Please visit our website, www.greenhavenpublishing.com. For a free color catalog of all our high-quality books, call toll free 1-844-317-7404 or fax 1-844-317-7405.

Contents

The development of drugs and drug use in America is a cultural paradox. On the one hand, strong, potentially dangerous drugs provide people with relief from numerous physical and psychological ailments. Sedatives such as Valium counter the effects of anxiety; steroids treat severe burns, anemia, and some forms of cancer; and morphine provides quick pain relief. On the other hand, many drugs (sedatives, steroids, and morphine among them) are consistently misused or abused. Millions of Americans struggle each year with drug addictions that overpower their ability to think and act rationally. Researchers often link drug abuse to criminal activity, traffic accidents, domestic violence, and suicide.

These harmful effects seem obvious today. Newspaper articles, medical journals, and scientific studies have highlighted the many problems drug use and abuse can cause. Yet, there was a time when many of the drugs now known to be harmful were actually believed to be beneficial. Cocaine, for example, was once hailed as a great cure, used to treat everything from nausea and weakness to colds and asthma. Developed in Europe during the 1880s, cocaine spread quickly to the United States, where manufacturers made it the primary ingredient in such everyday substances as cough medicines, lozenges, and tonics. Likewise, heroin, an opium derivative, became a popular painkiller during the late 19th century. Doctors and patients flocked to American drugstores to buy heroin, which was described as the optimal cure for even the worst coughs and chest pains.

As more people began using these drugs, though, doctors, legislators, and the public at large began to realize that they were more damaging than beneficial. After years of using heroin as a painkiller, for example, patients began asking their doctors for larger and stronger doses. Cocaine users reported dangerous side effects, including hallucinations and wild mood shifts. As a result, the U.S. government initiated more stringent regulation of many powerful and addictive drugs, and in some cases outlawed them entirely.

A drug's legal status is not always indicative of how dangerous it is, however. Some drugs known to have harmful effects can be purchased legally in the United States and elsewhere. Nicotine, a key ingredient in cigarettes, is known to be highly addictive. In an effort to meet their body's demand for nicotine, smokers expose themselves to lung cancer, emphysema, and other life-threatening conditions. Despite these risks, nicotine is legal almost everywhere.

Other drugs that cannot be purchased or sold legally are the subject of much debate regarding their effects on physical and mental health. Marijuana, sometimes described as a gateway drug that leads users to other drugs, cannot legally be used, grown, or sold in half of the United States. However, some research suggests that marijuana is neither addictive nor a gateway drug and that it might actually have a host of health benefits, which has led to its legalization in many states for medical use only. A handful of states also permit it to be used recreationally, but the debate on this matter still rages.

The Drug Education Library examines the paradox of drug use in America by focusing on some of the most commonly used and abused drugs or categories of drugs available today. By objectively discussing the many types of drugs, their intended purposes, their effects (both planned and unplanned), and the controversies surrounding them, the books in this series provide readers with an understanding of the complex role drugs play in American society. Informative sidebars, annotated bibliographies, and lists of organizations to contact add to the text and provide young readers with many opportunities for further discussion and research.

MARIJUANA: HERE TO STAY

Marijuana is the most commonly used illegal drug in the United States today. It was not always illegal; it has, in fact, been used around the world for thousands of years. Ancient Chinese doctors prescribed it for pain; writers and artists consumed it to enhance their creativity; and today it is still used for religious ceremonies in countries such as India and Jamaica. Although it is outlawed in most of the United States, not everyone believes this law is justified. In fact, in 2015, the Pew Research Center reported that about 151 million Americans have tried marijuana at least once in their lifetime. That is 49 percent of the population of the United States. This number has increased from 94 million, or 40 percent, since 2003.

Law enforcement has tried various methods of eradicating marijuana from our society, but without success. Proponents of legalization compare the anti-marijuana laws to Prohibition, the failed attempt to outlaw alcohol in the 1920s and early 1930s. From the start, the law was unpopular and widely violated. By the time Prohibition was finally repealed in 1933, few people could say it had served much of a purpose. Nevertheless, many state and federal lawmakers, as well as the courts, have been steadfast in making sure marijuana remains an illegal substance. Many states have decriminalized marijuana, meaning, according to the National Organization for the Reform of Marijuana Laws, that there is "typically ... no arrest, prison time, or criminal record for the first-time possession of a small amount of marijuana for personal consumption. In most decriminalized states, these offenses are treated like a minor traffic violation."[1] Some states have legalized the drug for medical purposes only, and four states have legalized it completely. However, where state and federal laws conflict, the federal one will always win out. The Supreme Court ruled in 2005 that, while it could be suggested that marijuana serves a legitimate medical use, the likelihood that the drug would be abused is just too great to risk legalizing it for any purpose. Therefore, marijuana remains illegal at the federal level everywhere in the United States. However, in 2009, the federal government issued a statement pledging that in states where marijuana is legal for medical or recreational use, the prosecution of individuals for these crimes will be a low priority. This effectively means that people who are following state guidelines for possession and use of marijuana will not be pursued by the federal government. Instead, the federal government targets dispensaries and drug dealers who sell marijuana to people who are not legally allowed to use it, including people under the age of 21 in states where it is legal for both medical and recreational use; non-patients in states where it is legal for medical use only; and anyone in states that have not legalized it for any purpose.

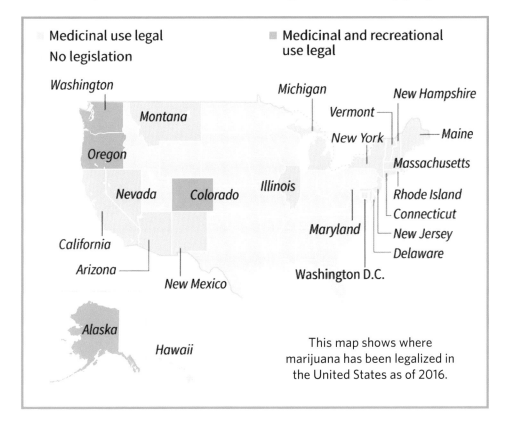

Medicinal use legal
No legislation

Medicinal and recreational use legal

Washington
Montana
Oregon
Nevada
Colorado
California
Arizona
New Mexico
Alaska
Hawaii

Michigan
Vermont
New York
Illinois
Maryland
Washington D.C.

New Hampshire
Maine
Massachusetts
Rhode Island
Connecticut
New Jersey
Delaware

This map shows where marijuana has been legalized in the United States as of 2016.

Some people oppose any form of legalization, even for medical purposes. They point to the numerous health consequences that have been attributed to marijuana—such as lung damage and loss of short-term memory—and argue vehemently against any effort to legalize the drug. Because it is classified a Schedule I drug, marijuana has not been extensively studied—the law makes it difficult for researchers to obtain the drug in order to test it. They must be granted a license from the Drug Enforcement Administration (DEA) and then request access to the National Institute on Drug Abuse's (NIDA) research supply. This request may be refused even after the license is obtained. For this reason, opponents of legalization remain unconvinced of marijuana's purported benefits.

Smokers from All Walks of Life

Marijuana is known by many names on the street, among them pot, grass, weed, and reefer. There is no question that the drug is a big part of youth culture. Rock stars and rappers sing about their experiences under the influence of the drug. Pot is readily available at concerts and parties. Each year on April 20, thousands of people gather to celebrate marijuana and smoking culture. In many people's minds, the typical marijuana smoker is the teenage stoner who gets high

Young people are not the only ones who smoke pot.

Marijuana is classified by the government as a Schedule I drug, which means there can be severe penalties for anyone who is caught growing, selling, or using it.

between classes or after school. However, that is a myth. A study conducted by NIDA in 2014 found that 16 percent of teenagers 17 and under admitted to using marijuana. Meanwhile, Gallup polls showed that 37 percent of people between the ages of 18 and 29 and 50 percent of people between the ages of 30 and 49 admitted to having smoked marijuana. As for people over 50, 71 percent said they had used marijuana at some point in their lives.

Importation on the Decline

Another reason marijuana remains a presence in American society is that it is the lone illegal drug that is both imported and produced domestically. Although accurate statistics are nearly impossible to find, since illegal growers and importers do not keep a public record of their stock, the Drug Policy Research Center estimated in 2008 that roughly one-third of all marijuana was grown secretly in America, while the majority was imported, mainly from Mexico. Thanks to the legalization of pot cultivation in some states, the *Los Angeles Times* reported in 2015 that it is believed importation from Mexico is on the decline.

Marijuana has turned out to be a drug with growing popularity. Judging by the millions of pot smokers from all ages and all walks of life, it would appear that many people are unconcerned about its use.

Chapter One

THE HISTORY OF MARIJUANA

Marijuana has a long and colorful history that dates back thousands of years. Some ancient texts refer to drugs that historians believe may be marijuana. The poet Homer wrote that Helen of Troy discovered the drug in Egypt and introduced it to her subjects. In the fifth century BC, Greek historian Herodotus wrote about the Scythians, who were inhabitants of an island in the Araxes River who would throw their cannabis leaves into a fire, then "sit around in a circle; and by inhaling the fruit that has been thrown on, they become intoxicated by the odor, just as the Greeks do by wine; and the more fruit that is thrown on, the more intoxicated they become, until they rise up and dance and betake themselves to singing."[2]

In botanical terms, "marijuana" actually refers to the flowers and leafy parts of the plant known as *Cannabis sativa*, although for legal purposes, "marijuana" often refers to the entire plant. The chemical that gives marijuana its narcotic effect is delta-9-tetrahydrocannabinol, or THC. The chemical is found in the flowers and leaves of the plant and not in the stalk, which is the fibrous portion of cannabis.

The resin that can be extracted from the plant is rich in THC. When compressed into a paste, the resin is known as hashish or hash. One dose of hashish, which is typically smoked in a pipe, is said to have five to eight times the potency of a marijuana cigarette, commonly known as a joint.

There are two types of cannabis plants. The kind we call marijuana contains THC and other compounds that, when smoked, give the user a high. The other kind is known as hemp, although both types of cannabis are forms of the hemp plant. Hemp con-

The leaves and flowers of the cannabis plant are known as marijuana, but the whole plant is illegal in many states.

tains almost no THC and has many industrial uses. Both are considered Schedule I drugs, which the DEA defines as "drugs with no currently accepted medical use and a high potential for abuse."[3] Other Schedule I drugs include heroin, LSD, and Ecstasy. There are high penalties for being caught using, selling, or transporting these drugs.

In addition to the two types of cannabis, there are two strains of marijuana called sativa and indica. They have different ratios of THC to CBD (cannabidiol), which produces different effects on the mind and body. Sativas are higher in THC than CBD, making the user feel "high"—thoughts race and the body feels energized. Indicas are the opposite, producing a "stoned" feeling—sleepy and numb, with slowed-down thought processes. For medical use, sativas are more commonly chosen to stimulate hunger in chemotherapy or AIDS patients, while indicas are used to relieve pain, muscle spasms, and insomnia.

Cannabis in the New World

In the 1200s, Marco Polo wrote about an Arab prince who fed marijuana to his guards to enhance their courage. Other explorers who visited Asia and the Middle East brought the plant back with them, introducing cannabis to the European countries. Cannabis became a valuable crop, both as hemp and marijuana. European writers were particularly enthusiastic about marijuana; in 1844, some of the top authors in Paris—including Victor Hugo, Honoré de Balzac, and Alexandre Dumas—established *Le Club des Hashischins*, where they could share their hashish while pursuing their creative interests.

Cannabis arrived in America with the Jamestown, Virginia, settlers in 1607. The settlers grew the plant because they needed hemp to make their own clothes since supply ships from Europe were infrequent visitors to the colony. In fact, the hemp crop was so valuable that colonial governments eventually ordered farmers to grow it, fining them if they refused.

The evidence suggests that while the colonial hemp farmers did know cannabis could also produce a narcotic effect, few of them were known to be pot smokers. George Washington, for example, grew hemp on his Virginia farm. Washington's diary entries report that he destroyed the leafy parts of the plant, causing historians to conclude that the founding father had no interest in consuming his crop.

Marijuana Use Before Its Prohibition

Still, by the 1800s, many Americans were using marijuana for recreational purposes. It was occasionally smoked, but at the time, most marijuana users achieved their highs by chewing and even eating the leaves. The more prosperous users could afford to visit secret hash parlors, where they smoked hashish in elaborate Arabian pipes known as hookahs that filtered the harsh smoke through water. These have become popular again in recent years, but hookah bars in the United States today only offer their customers tobacco. In 1883, Dr. H. H. Kane described his experience in a New York City hash den to the readers of *Harper's New Monthly Magazine*. The hash smokers, he wrote, "are about evenly divided between Americans and foreigners; indeed, the place is kept by a Greek, who has invested a great deal of money in it. All the visitors, both male and female, are of the better classes, and absolute secrecy is the rule. The house has been opened about two years, I believe, and the number of regular habitués is daily on the increase."[4]

At the time, marijuana and hashish were not illegal drugs in America. Although the rise of the cotton industry in the 1800s had made hemp a much less important fabric, cannabis was still widely grown on farm fields throughout the country. In fact, in 1914, Congress passed the Harrison Narcotic Act, outlawing the use of most drugs for recreational purposes. Marijuana was omitted from the law at the request of the hemp farmers.

The War on Marijuana

Nevertheless, there was widespread belief among many leaders of society and government that marijuana caused trouble. In 1915, California became the first state to outlaw recreational use of marijuana. Wyoming followed the same year. By 1937, all but 2 of the 48 states had passed laws banning marijuana.

When resin from the cannabis plant is compressed into a paste, it is known as hashish.

In most cases, the state legislatures were prompted to act after newspapers reported sensational crime stories in which the perpetrators admitted to being high on marijuana. Stories such as this one from Universal News Service were typical of the time:

> *Shocking crimes of violence are increasing. Murders, slaughterings, cruel mutilations, maimings, done in cold blood, as if some hideous monster was amok in the land.*
>
> *Alarmed Federal and State authorities attribute much of this violence to the "killer drug."*
>
> *That's what experts call marihuana [marijuana]. It is another name for hashish. It's a derivative of Indian hemp, a roadside weed in almost every State of the Union ...*
>
> *Those addicted to marihuana, after an early feeling of exhilaration, soon lose all restraints, all inhibitions. They become bestial demoniacs, filled with the mad lust to kill.*[5]

In 1927, a campaign by newspapers in New Orleans prompted the Louisiana legislature to outlaw marijuana. Within days of the law's adoption, a New Orleans newspaper reported a wholesale arrest of more than 150 people: "Approximately one hundred underworld dives, soft-drink establishments, night clubs, grocery stores, and private homes were searched in the police raids. Addicts, hardened criminals, gangsters, women of the streets, sailors of all nationalities, bootleggers, boys and girls—many flashily dressed in silks and furs, others in working clothes—all were rounded up in the net."[6] Other states began to ban it one by one.

Still, at this time using or selling marijuana was not a federal crime. Throughout this period, Congress was much more concerned with abuse of alcohol than with drugs. This was the era that saw the rise of the temperance movement. Activists such as Carrie Nation were making the headlines by leading protests against saloons. Finally, the dry movement had its way, and in 1920, the 18th Amendment to the Constitution became law, making it illegal to sell and buy alcoholic beverages in America.

Prohibition, which lasted 13 years, was largely a failure. Mobsters took over the beer and liquor business, smuggling it into the United States from other countries or manufacturing it in underground breweries and distilleries on American soil. The taverns may have been boarded up, but illegal clubs known as speakeasies opened for business. It is estimated that during the height of Prohibition, some 200,000 speakeasies were in operation.

Along with the speakeasies, illegal tearooms opened for business in New Orleans. The rooms served a potent tea brewed from marijuana leaves or simply sold marijuana cigarettes to their customers for prices as low as 25 cents per joint. Mostly, the tearooms were found in poor black neighborhoods in inner cities. It is believed that no fewer than 500 tearooms operated in the mostly black New York City neighborhood of Harlem in the 1930s.

During the 1920s, the government was more concerned with arresting people who drank alcohol than those who smoked marijuana.

With Prohibition nearing its repeal, Congress turned its attention to illegal drugs, establishing the Federal Bureau of Narcotics in 1930. The bureau's first director, Harry J. Anslinger, called for a federal law banning marijuana. He got his way with the adoption of the Marihuana Tax Act of 1937, which assessed fees on anyone who grew, sold, or prescribed marijuana. The fees themselves were small, but the process for paying them was made intentionally difficult, and the penalties for failing to file the correct paperwork were prohibitively high. During World War II, hemp was grown in abundance because all raw materials

A CULT CLASSIC

Marijuana does not cause mental illness, but for years many people were under the impression that the drug could cause depression and even insanity, thanks to the 1936 film *Reefer Madness*. The movie tells the outlandish story of college students who become homicidal and suicidal after consuming pot.

The movie was originally titled *Tell Your Children*. Produced by a church group to serve as an educational film for parents, the film tried to warn adults of the dangers of pot. However, independent film producer Dwain Esper obtained the film, reedited it, and added new scenes. Esper made the story more dramatic and renamed the film *Reefer Madness*.

The film tells what happens to a group of students after they consume marijuana. One character, Bill, suffers from hallucinations. His girlfriend, Blanche, commits suicide. Another student, Ralph, goes insane, commits a murder, and is sentenced to an asylum.

Today, *Reefer Madness* is a cult classic. It is shown mostly on college campuses and theaters that specialize in screening art films.

were much in demand; farmers could apply for tax stamps that allowed them to avoid paying the fees. Following the war, the tax was ruled unconstitutional, and marijuana was added to the list of illegal drugs instead. No distinction was made between marijuana and hemp; all forms of the cannabis plant were outlawed.

Anslinger's agents made nearly 400 arrests within the first four months the law was on the books. The Bureau of Narcotics would carry on its war against marijuana for a few more years, but in 1941, America's attention was diverted to a much different war. With American troops fighting fascism in Europe and the Pacific, enforcement of the laws against marijuana abuse was hardly a national priority. When World War II ended in 1945, the troops came home to marry their sweethearts, start new lives, and raise their families in comfortable suburban housing developments.

The Underground Pot Movement

Not quite everyone sought that lifestyle, however. Some of the men who returned home from the war had other ideas. They gravitated to New York's Greenwich Village and other hip city neighborhoods, where they and their girlfriends lived in tiny flats and spent their evenings in dimly lit coffeehouses. That lifestyle would lead to the rise of the so-called Beat Generation in the 1950s. Their heroes were writers Jack Kerouac, Allen Ginsberg, and William S. Burroughs. The Beats wrote poetry, listened to jazz, and smoked marijuana. New York writer Dan Wakefield recalled meeting Ginsberg in 1961 while researching a magazine story about marijuana:

> When I went to interview him, which I did several times, Allen opened a big file cabinet and pulled out reports for me to read on the medical, legal, and historical aspects of cannabis sativa. He was eager to help anyone who would write objectively about this drug he believed should be legalized, offering facts and opinions and background information, all in a friendly,

matter-of-fact manner. To my great relief, he did not use jargon or hip lingo ("Like, you know, I was uptight that he might jive me, but he was cool"), nor was he ever stoned when I talked with him, a possibility I also feared.

Explaining the role of marijuana to the poets of his own circle, he told me that "almost everyone has experimented with it and tried writing something [while] on it. It's all part of their poetic—no, their metaphysical—education." [7]

Young people in the 1950s and 1960s considered their use of marijuana to be a rebellion against authority.

Wakefield concluded that marijuana "was moving from the back rooms of jazz bars and coldwater pads of hipsters in Harlem and the East Village, seeping through the walls of college dormitories and into middle-class consciousness."[8] It certainly was. Within a few years, the 1960s had erupted into an era of dramatic social change, and marijuana was definitely at the center of the counterculture movement.

College students rebelled against the authority of their parents and teachers. Campuses became hotbeds of radical thought. Students protested against the Vietnam War, but they also demonstrated in favor of civil rights, women's rights, and free speech. Thousands of "hippies" and "flower children" flocked to San Francisco's Haight-Ashbury district and other urban neighborhoods where illegal drug use was rampant. Young people used drugs in defiance of authority. Essayist Andrew Peyton Thomas wrote, "For the flower children, of course, the marijuana leaf was the emblem of a generation mutinying against parental authority and self-restraint."[9]

Marijuana promised a mellow, feel-good high that could deliver an escape from the hassles of school, the police, or the weighty issues of the day. Marijuana smoke wafted freely at rock concerts and campus demonstrations. At the Woodstock Music and Arts Festival in upstate New York, the *New York Times* reported that no less than 99 percent of the crowd of 400,000 concertgoers smoked marijuana during the 3-day event in August 1969. The newspaper reported:

A billowy haze of sweet smoke rose through purple spotlights from the sloping hillside where throngs of young people—their average age about 20—sat or sprawled in the midnight darkness and listened to the rock music.

The smoke was not from the campfires.

"There was so much grass being smoked last night that you could get stoned just sitting there breathing," said a 19-year-old student from Denison University in Ohio. "It got so you didn't even want another drag of anything."[10]

The concertgoers were not concerned with being punished for their actions. "They smoked quite openly, not fearing to be 'busted,' at least not within the confines of the 600-acre farm where the action is,"[11] the *Times* added. In fact, spokesmen for the New York State Police told reporters that they made few narcotics arrests that weekend. One festivalgoer who slipped through their grasp was the bass player for the band Country Joe and the Fish, who flashed his joint at a camera filming a documentary. Another headliner was folk singer Arlo Guthrie, who performed "Coming into Los Angeles" on the Woodstock stage. The song told the story of smuggling two kilograms of marijuana through the U.S. customs inspection station at Los Angeles Airport. The song turned out to be a big hit for Guthrie.

Marijuana Goes Mainstream

Marijuana did not stay in the counterculture for long. Starting in the 1960s, savvy entrepreneurs established so-called head shops that sold all kinds of drug paraphernalia to their hippie clients. Among the products found in the shops were colorful and flavored cigarette papers, which were needed by do-it-yourselfers to roll their own joints; glass pipes, known as bongs; and roach clips, which could hold the final remnants of a joint so that the marijuana smoke could be inhaled without burning one's fingers. By the 1970s, the head shops had moved out of cluttered inner city neighborhoods and into suburban shopping centers. In describing her neighborhood head shop, Tela Ropa in Pittsburgh, writer Kristy Graver said, "Local high school kids flocked to Tela Ropa like stoners to a bag of Doritos. Before you could say 'peace-love-dope,' they blew their lunch money on incense, lava lamps and candles shaped like marijuana leaves."[12]

Laws Become Stricter

Authorities fretted over the shops, but there was little they could do. The state governments had outlawed marijuana, and the federal government had acted as well. In 1956, the U.S. Narcotics Control Act set a minimum sentence of two years in prison for

UNINTENDED CONSEQUENCES

In 1969, the federal government conceived a plan to stop the flow of marijuana across the Mexican border. The plan, known as Operation Intercept, required U.S. customs agents to inspect every car, truck, and bus that stopped at each of the 30 border crossings located along the 2,500-mile (4,000 km) Mexico-U.S. border.

The program was launched on September 21, 1969. Each day, thousands of vehicles were stopped and searched. Initially, the program produced dramatic results. In America, a genuine pot shortage developed. One Radcliffe College student told the *Wall Street Journal* that she switched to LSD because it was so hard to find marijuana. Said the student: "I really didn't want to try acid before, but there's no grass around, so when somebody offered me some [LSD], I figured, 'What the hell.' I didn't freak out or anything, so I've been tripping [taking LSD] ever since."[1]

Operation Intercept was halted after just 20 days. Officials were concerned that the lack of marijuana prompted drug users like the Radcliffe student to turn to harsher substances. Also, the searches caused tremendous traffic jams at the border crossings; motorists had to wait more than two hours for customs agents to search their vehicles. More importantly, the economy on the American side suffered. Because of the long wait at the customs stations, Mexican laborers refused to cross the border to go to their jobs in America.

1. Quoted in Edward M. Brecher, *Licit and Illicit Drugs.* Mount Vernon, NY: Consumers Union, 1972, p. 435.

marijuana possession, although in 1970, the United States Controlled Substances Act eliminated federal jail sentences for the possession of small amounts of marijuana. (Mandatory minimum sentences were reinstated by a law enacted in 1986.) Still, the paraphernalia of the drug trade had not been regulated by either the federal or state governments.

In the early 1970s, states started passing laws prohibiting the sale of drug paraphernalia. Head shop owners were arrested, but when their cases got to court, the charges were dismissed and the laws overruled. Courts ruled that the laws were too vague and did not specifically identify a glass pipe or roach clip as an illegal item. Indeed, most states adopted laws that merely suggested if an item could be used for the consumption of marijuana, it was illegal. Under the laws in existence at the time, the shop owners could claim that the paraphernalia had a legitimate use—every pipe, paper, bong, and roach clip on the shelves could also

These colorful pipes are often used to smoke marijuana.

be used to smoke tobacco, which was legal everywhere. Judges agreed and threw out the cases against the head shop owners.

In 1979, the DEA drafted a model law that identified bongs, roach clips, and similar items as employed specifically for consumption of drugs. States adopted the model laws, and in 1999, Congress passed sweeping legislation making the manufacture and sale of drug paraphernalia federal offenses punishable by up to three years in prison.

Many head shops as well as the manufacturers of paraphernalia managed to remain in business for years after the laws were adopted. As small businesses operating on the periphery of the drug trade, they were hardly regarded as priorities for police and prosecutors, who were more concerned with the growing traffic in crack cocaine and methamphetamine. Meanwhile, with the growth of the Internet, paraphernalia dealers and manufacturers could remain in business while hiding behind anonymous websites. In 2003, the United States Department of Justice announced a crackdown on head shops and paraphernalia manufacturers. A program titled Operation Pipe Dreams led to the arrests of dozens of paraphernalia makers and dealers. However, only one person was charged—Tommy Chong, an actor known for playing a bumbling pothead in several movies in the 1970s. His conviction was intended to serve as an example to other paraphernalia sellers. Aside from this arrest, the operation was largely ineffective, and although the law remains on the books, it is rare for head shops to be targeted.

A Change in Attitude

As Operation Pipe Dreams shows, decades after marijuana was first outlawed, authorities must still work very hard to keep the drug out of American society. The fact is, though, that they have largely failed. State governments are starting to come around to the idea that they will never be able to eradicate it, and some have chosen to legalize it so they can better control its sale and share in the profits by taxing it. Preliminary studies have shown that pot can alleviate symptoms of certain medical conditions, but like prescription pills or alcohol, the potential for abuse is still

POT SMOKERS IN THE MEDIA

The common perception of someone who smokes marijuana frequently—generally known as a pothead or stoner—is of an always cheerful, slow-thinking, forgetful young adult. Movies such as *Dazed and Confused*, *Dude, Where's My Car?*, and *Harold and Kumar Go to White Castle* showcase these stereotypes. However, some movies and TV shows have begun to show that pot smokers can have very diverse personalities. On *That 70s Show*, a group of friends was routinely shown getting high together. While high, they all appeared to act in the same manner, but when they are sober, they had different reactions to the same situations, showing that it is not always easy to tell who smokes pot. The TV show *Weeds* centered on a suburban mom who starts growing and selling pot illegally to pay off her debt. This show was a comedy but featured a darker depiction of the types of people who use and sell marijuana. It highlighted the violence and rivalry between different growing operations.

Harold and Kumar Go to White Castle showcases the stereotype that stoners become obsessed with food when they get high.

present. Frequent marijuana smokers face an unfortunate truth: There are some very real and dangerous health risks involved in pursuing their habit. For example, medical research has shown that smoking marijuana irritates the respiratory system, just like smoking tobacco. Young adults who use marijuana heavily may be at risk for permanent memory impairment, decreased IQ, and increased risk for testicular cancer in males.

Chapter Two

THE PHYSICAL AND MENTAL EFFECTS OF MARIJUANA

Marijuana smokers experience the euphoria of a dreamy high that begins within minutes of the drug entering their lungs. Typically, they are stoned for two hours or more, then the effect of the drug wears off. Of course, the more they smoke, the longer they stay high, and consuming the drug in edible form makes the high last about twice as long.

Joe L. (name changed) has been smoking pot illegally for years. He started in high school because his friends offered him some and he was curious. He enjoys the feeling of being high and does not feel that he has experienced any ill effects or addiction, "but I can easily see how it could be used as a crutch."[13]

One problem with determining the effects of marijuana is that weed that is grown today contains more THC than it did 20 years ago. As previously mentioned, the fact that pot is a Schedule I drug makes performing scientific studies difficult, but even the ones that have been done may not be completely accurate anymore due to the increased potency. Any positive effects may not apply anymore, and any negative effects will be heightened due to the increase in the amount of chemicals being absorbed.

One recent study by Northwestern Medicine reported that teenagers who used the drug even occasionally "showed significant abnormalities in two key brain regions that are important in emotion and motivation."[14] The more they smoked, the more significant these changes became, and the effects persisted up to two years after they stopped using pot. The dangers of occasional recreational use drop after age 21, when the brain has fully developed, although older frequent users sometimes report that they have problems with memory, multitasking, and thinking clearly.

Changes in the Brain

When marijuana smoke is inhaled, the fumes carry the chemical THC into the lungs. The THC comes to rest on the millions of alveoli that line the lungs. These are tiny sacs that absorb oxygen and pass it into the bloodstream. Of course, whatever is mixed in with the oxygen is passed into the bloodstream as well. After being inhaled, it takes only seconds for the THC to reach the blood.

Marijuana can also be eaten. Generally, butter or oil is infused with pot and baked into food such as brownies or cupcakes. When the food is digested, the THC enters the blood through the lining of the stomach. It takes longer for THC to be absorbed through the stomach, but once it enters the blood, the effect is stronger and lasts longer than smoking.

The blood courses through the human body and eventually finds its way into the brain. That is where the THC comes into contact with neurotransmitters, the chemicals that deliver messages from brain cell to brain cell, affecting human behavior.

Brain cells are known as neurons; each person has millions. Each neuron emits electrical impulses containing messages that control the body's functions. To leave the neurons, impulses travel along large stems known as axons and smaller stems known as dendrites. When an impulse reaches the end of an axon, it will jump over a tiny space known as a synapse on its journey to the dendrite of the next neuron. When the electrical signal makes the jump, the brain cell releases a neurotransmitter chemical to carry the message. Accepting the message on the end of the dendrite is a group of molecules known as receptors. These receptors can only accept specific neurotransmitters. This is how the neurons of the brain work together to tell a foot to take a step, a hand to hold a pencil, or the lips to form words so that a person may speak. Not all neurotransmitters carry messages. Some neurotransmitters block unwanted messages from jumping from cell to cell.

A drug will influence the transmission of information from neuron to neuron. The drug may produce a flood of neurotransmitters so that too many messages are delivered to the neurons; it may neutralize the neurotransmitters that work to block unwanted information, causing a flood of unwanted messages to reach the neurons; or the drug may act as its own neurotransmitter, sending its own messages to the brain cells.

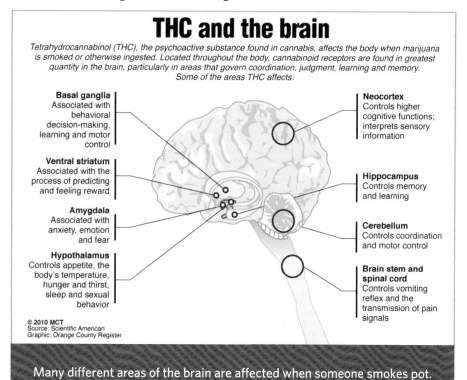

THC and the brain

Tetrahydrocannabinol (THC), the psychoactive substance found in cannabis, affects the body when marijuana is smoked or otherwise ingested. Located throughout the body, cannabinoid receptors are found in greatest quantity in the brain, particularly in areas that govern coordination, judgment, learning and memory. Some of the areas THC affects:

Basal ganglia
Associated with behavioral decision-making, learning and motor control

Ventral striatum
Associated with the process of predicting and feeling reward

Amygdala
Associated with anxiety, emotion and fear

Hypothalamus
Controls appetite, the body's temperature, hunger and thirst, sleep and sexual behavior

Neocortex
Controls higher cognitive functions; interprets sensory information

Hippocampus
Controls memory and learning

Cerebellum
Controls coordination and motor control

Brain stem and spinal cord
Controls vomiting reflex and the transmission of pain signals

© 2010 MCT
Source: Scientific American
Graphic: Orange County Register

Many different areas of the brain are affected when someone smokes pot.

When THC enters the brain, it bonds with the neurotransmitter anandamide. The combination of the two chemicals has been found to affect behavior in a number of ways. For example, as the combination of anandamide and THC jumps from neuron to neuron, it causes loss of short-term memory.

THC in low doses also promotes the brain's release of the neurotransmitter serotonin, giving pot smokers the dreamy, lightheaded, mellow high for which marijuana is known. As the effects wear off and the serotonin leaves the system, people may feel unhappy or tired. Smoking too much can cause the reverse effect, inhibiting serotonin to cause depression and increased risk of psychosis in people who are already genetically predisposed to it.

THC is not the only chemical contained in marijuana smoke that causes changes in the body and the brain. In fact, marijuana smoke contains approximately 400 different chemicals, many of which alter neurotransmitters. Some of them enhance the effect of the THC on the neurotransmitters, while others affect the brain and body in their own ways. Some of those chemicals cause an increase in pulse rate, while others are known to cause anxiety and panic attacks.

The Risk of Addiction

Many marijuana smokers are known to stick with the drug for years. In the brain, one of the neurotransmitters affected by THC is dopamine, which creates feelings of well-being. This is why people feel happy while they are high and why they want to try it again. The stimulated flow of dopamine helps create addiction in users. Recent research has also shown that marijuana abuse can cause people to react less strongly to dopamine when they are not high, permanently impairing the ability to react to pleasurable experiences and leading to a constant general feeling of irritability.

For years, scientists questioned whether marijuana was addictive, but recent studies have indicated that pot can truly cause its users to come back for more. Joseph Rey, Andres Martin, and Peter Krabman cited a study in which 12 marijuana smokers consumed the drug regularly for 16 consecutive days, then were asked to stop. They found that people who were asked to give up pot cold turkey exhibited symptoms similar to cigarette smokers who suddenly find themselves without their daily dose of nicotine. They wrote:

Irritability, restlessness, anger, and sleep problems increased significantly on cessation of use. This is consistent with oth-

er studies, reports by young people in residential care who were marijuana dependent, findings in community surveys, and laboratory studies. Thus, the symptoms and intensity of withdrawal in severe marijuana users appear clinically significant and are not dissimilar to those observed during nicotine withdrawal.[15]

The risk of developing cannabis dependence syndrome is greater for people under the age of 18.

Marijuana not only creates a physical addiction in its users but a psychological dependence as well. This means that pot smokers rely on the drug to lift their mood and help them get through the day. Psychologists call this condition cannabis dependence syndrome. As many as 30 percent of long-term smokers of marijuana are believed to suffer from the syndrome. Chronic users find they need larger and larger doses to achieve the high they seek. According to NIDA, "People who begin using marijuana before the age of 18 are four to seven times more likely to develop a marijuana use disorder than adults."[16]

Christopher (name changed) was one such teen. He began smoking in high school and continued through his mid-20s. Soon he found that he was addicted:

> In my experience, any habit can become an addiction. When habits get out of control, they become addictions. In times, places, and situations where I would often smoke, that behavior developed into a reflex. It wasn't a decision anymore. I didn't have cravings, but I did have withdrawal. I was stressed out more and would get agitated more easily, which was not normal for me. The only way to get over it was to completely remove myself from circumstances that would lead to that reflex. But I couldn't have done it without the support and understanding of my friends. Your friends won't realize you have a problem unless you tell them.[17]

Physical Impairment

In addition to causing memory loss, the combination of THC and anandamide has another significant impact on the body: loss of coordination. That is why pot smokers often stumble around and bump into things. THC's effect on coordination can create a dangerous situation if somebody who is stoned gets behind the wheel of a car.

In 2000, the United States National Highway Traffic Safety Administration examined issues surrounding drug abuse and driving at a conference in Seattle, Washington. The conference was composed of toxicologists, who are scientists that study the effects of chemicals and other substances on the human body and human performance. The toxicologists studied 16 drugs and similar substances, including some that are legally available as over-the-counter medications, as well as drugs available only through prescriptions. Several illegal drugs, including marijuana, were also studied. The toxicologists conducted the study to determine whether people under the influence of those drugs could safely operate motor vehicles. The conclusion reached by the toxicologists was that users of marijuana should not drive, particularly when the drug is used in combination with alcohol. In their report for the Highway Traffic Safety Administration, the toxicologists wrote that marijuana

> has been shown to impair performance on driving simulator tasks and on open and closed driving courses for up to approximately three hours. Decreased car handling performance, increased reaction times, impaired time and distance estimation, inability to maintain headway, lateral travel, subjective sleepiness ... and impaired sustained vigilance have all been reported ... The greater demands placed on the driver ... the more critical the likely impairment. Marijuana may particularly impair monotonous and prolonged driving. Decision times to evaluate situations and determine appropriate responses increase. Mixing alcohol and marijuana may dramatically produce effects greater than either drug on its own.[18]

The toxicologists concluded that "low doses of THC moderately impair cognitive and psychomotor tasks associated with driving, while severe driving impairment is observed with high doses, chronic use and in combination with low doses of alcohol. The more difficult and unpredictable the task, the more likely marijuana will impair performance."[19]

Despite this danger, people who consistently smoke marijuana can be found on the highways. Newspapers routinely report incidents in which drivers under the influence of the drug get into accidents, often killing innocent victims. These stories reported in the news include the case of Ralph Tarchine, 18,

METHODS OF DETECTING MARIJUANA

It takes anywhere from three days to four weeks for traces of THC to leave the system following the last use of the drug. This depends on many factors, including how frequently the person smokes, how fast the person's metabolism is, whether the pot was smoked or eaten, how much of it was taken, and how sensitive the test is. Head shops often sell detox products that claim to flush the marijuana out of a person's system quickly in case of a surprise drug test. However, these drinks and pills are generally ineffective.

Marijuana can be detected in the body through urine, blood, hair, or saliva. A urine test is the most commonly administered method. Infrequent users will generally fail if they are tested within three days of their last use; the more frequent the use, the longer it takes the body to completely purge the drug. A test of hair follicles can detect its presence up to 90 days after the last use, but this test is less commonly used because it takes longer for the drug to appear in the hair than in the urine. It is generally used to test long-term use, while a urine test is used to determine occasional or recent use.

In recent years, members of high school and college sports teams have been expected to take drug tests. Many corporations now require job applicants to pass drug tests. Also, police officers, prison guards, and others who work in law enforcement are often expected to take regular drug tests.

of White Plains, New York, who was charged in two accidents linked to marijuana and alcohol. In December 2005, Tarchine was charged with criminally negligent homicide when his car crashed, killing a 17-year-old passenger. Six weeks later, while Tarchine was out on bail, he smashed his car into a utility pole, crushing his legs. He was hospitalized for a month. According to prosecutors, Tarchine smoked marijuana before the first accident, then consumed alcohol before the second.

In Lake Worth, Florida, 45-year-old Michael Smith was allegedly under the influence of marijuana in 2006 when his car struck a woman and her two children, killing all three victims. Also in 2006, 17-year-old Curtis Clahassey pleaded guilty to driving under the influence and causing the death of another driver, 59-year-old Jerome Ratajczak. Police said Clahassey had been smoking marijuana, then lost control of his car, which crossed over the center line and struck Ratajczak's vehicle. Clahassey planned to start college in the fall of 2006, but he had to put those plans on hold while he served a year in jail. "This is a tragedy all around,"[20] said Kent County, Michigan, circuit judge Donald Johnston, who sentenced Clahassey.

Now that marijuana is legal in some states, the number of drug-related crashes is increasing. The AAA Foundation for Traffic Safety reports that in Washington State, which has legalized the drug, the number of fatal marijuana-related accidents has doubled. People in those states feel less worried about being under the influence in public now that they know they will not be arrested simply for having marijuana in their system, which may lead them to be less vigilant about safe behaviors. Like alcohol, there is a legal limit for the levels of THC in drivers' blood, but the current tests are often unreliable, making it difficult to legally determine if crashes are caused because of impairment or simple carelessness.

Long-Term Health Risks

Marijuana users may start coming down from their highs after two hours or so, but the marijuana stays in their body much

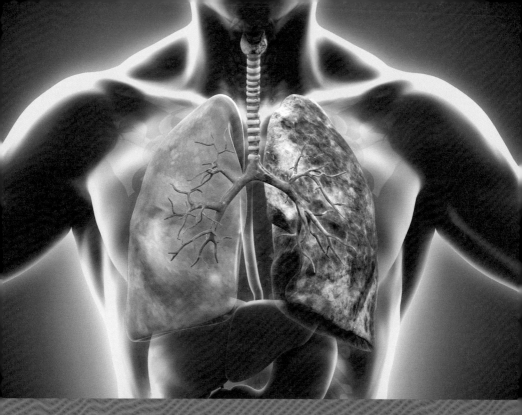

Frequent marijuana smokers are at risk for conditions such as bronchitis and asthma.

longer. That is why drug tests reveal marijuana use several days after the drug is consumed.

However, marijuana's impact on the human body does not stop after 10 days. The side effects of the drug can last much longer. Marijuana smoke contains tar, the sticky substance in cigarette smoke that sticks to the inside of the lungs, as well as other carcinogens. Heavy smokers of marijuana risk ailments commonly found among tobacco smokers—bronchitis, emphysema, and bronchial asthma. However, no proof has yet been found linking marijuana to lung cancer.

There is considerable debate over whether marijuana smokers are more or less likely to develop these conditions than tobacco smokers. Those who say it is more likely cite the fact that pot smokers tend to inhale more deeply and hold the smoke in their lungs longer than tobacco smokers do. Those who say it is less likely point out that marijuana users often smoke far less often than tobacco users. Consuming marijuana in edible or pill form significantly reduces the risk of developing one of these respiratory conditions.

The jazz trumpet player and singer Louis Armstrong smoked marijuana for years before his death in 1971. Eventually, the drug robbed him of his ability to blow into his horn. Armstrong's biographer, Laurence Bergreen, said:

> *This is one of the more difficult things about him to understand. He always said that he was old enough to remember when booze was illegal and pot was legal because of course he came of age in the Prohibition era in the 1920s. And the idea was—and he was not wholly mistaken at the time—that it was healthy. Well, it was healthier than toxic moonshine, which was making other jazz musicians sick and even killing them. And he felt that it relaxed him a lot. So even though he got into trouble with the law a few years later for possession of marijuana, he continued to use it in very heavy quantities, you know, three cigar-sized joints a day, at least, throughout his life.*
>
> *Now, this did have a long-term harmful effect. I think if you talk to a doctor, they'll tell you that that amount of heavy, chronic marijuana use will have a bad effect on your lungs, for starters, and Louis did indeed suffer lung problems in his last, later years and couldn't blow for a long period as a result.*[21]

Women who smoke tobacco are urged to give up cigarettes if they are pregnant because the chemicals in tobacco smoke can affect the fetus. Pregnant women who smoke marijuana face similar risks. The chemicals in marijuana smoke can enhance the possibility of premature delivery. Studies show that women who smoke pot increase the risk of pregnancy complications, including low birth weight or even stillbirth, meaning the baby dies in the womb. Also, marijuana smoke can affect the development of the brain of a baby still in its mother's womb. Psychologist Peter A. Fried of Ottawa, Canada, conducted studies on the effects of marijuana on young children. He found that the newborn babies of pot-smoking mothers tremble quite frequently and are easily startled. He also concluded that by the time the children of pot-smoking mothers reach the age of four, they suffer from reduced verbal ability, decreased attentiveness, increased impulsiveness, and shorter memories. "On tests of verbal ability and memory, the children of regular marijuana users were significantly inferior to other children,"[22] he wrote.

Experts are still unsure whether or not smoking marijuana leads to the use of harder drugs, such as crack cocaine.

Does Pot Lead to Harder Drug Use?

For years, sociologists, physicians, and psychologists have debated whether marijuana is a gateway drug, meaning it could eventually lead to the use of much harder drugs, such as methamphetamine, cocaine, and heroin. There is still not enough research to say conclusively whether this is true, but there are several theories on both sides. One school of thought holds that marijuana is a gateway drug because the street dealers who supply the pot to their customers are often in the business of selling other drugs. Therefore, the dealers encourage their pot customers to experiment with harder drugs, as well.

Additionally, as discussed earlier, frequent marijuana abuse decreases sensitivity to dopamine, especially when that use starts in adolescence. This may cause young adults with cannabis dependence syndrome to turn to harder drugs, looking for the good feeling they are no longer able to achieve. However, it is believed that infrequent use does not have the same effect, which means weed is not a gateway drug for adults who use it for medical purposes or occasional recreation. Joe L. feels that pot is only a gateway drug when it is illegal: "If weed is demonized, people may try it and find out they enjoy it. Then they might think all drugs are okay."[23] As with alcohol, moderation is key, and adolescents should abstain altogether to avoid weed's damaging effects, which are increased when the brain is still developing.

There is evidence to suggest that there is a higher correlation of marijuana users going on to other drugs, but correlation does not imply causation. This means that just because two things occur, it does not necessarily mean that one caused the other. For example, a person who uses both marijuana and cocaine may do so because their friends use both, not because using pot made them want to try cocaine. In fact, NIDA reports that, "the majority of people who use marijuana do not go on to use other, 'harder' substances."[24] Those who do may have a genetic predisposition to addictive behaviors or may often find themselves in social situations where hard drugs are used.

THE DANGERS OF SYNTHETIC CANNABINOIDS

In recent years, a type of drug has become available that combines dried, shredded herbs with synthetic, or man-made, chemicals that mimic the compounds in marijuana, such as THC and CBD. The chemicals are sprayed onto the plants, and users can then smoke them the same way they smoke weed. For this reason, the drug is sometimes called synthetic marijuana, fake pot, or legal weed, and it has brand names such as Spice or K2. It is illegal to produce or possess some of the chemicals used in synthetic cannabinoids, but since they are made in a lab, the creators try to get around the laws by changing their formulas to include legal ingredients. This is why they sometimes market their product as a legal alternative to marijuana and why it can be purchased in some head shops or gas stations.

Regardless of whether the chemicals in a given batch are legal or illegal, synthetic cannabinoids are extremely dangerous, although they are claimed to be safe alternatives to weed. They produce effects that are similar to marijuana, but stronger. They include hallucinations, confusion, extreme paranoia and anxiety, rapid heart rate, and seizures. Synthetic cannabinoids can be addictive and

Synthetic cannabinoids are more dangerous than pot.

produce withdrawal symptoms similar to those experienced by people going through marijuana withdrawal. These products are unregulated by the government, so as with drugs such as methamphetamines and LSD, users may never be completely sure what chemicals they are inhaling. Unlike marijuana, there is no evidence of health benefits from these drugs.

The Changing Weed Scene

Now that marijuana is legal for medical use in 25 states and the District of Columbia, as well as for recreational use in 4 of those 25, the way people view marijuana is changing. People who smoked pot used to be called losers and burnouts, and they were seen as being incapable of contributing to society. Today, many respectable people are open about their recreational drug use, and the majority of legally purchased marijuana is used by people whose doctors prescribed it to help them manage physical or mental ailments. In many states, it is legal for individuals to grow their own marijuana plants, although there are restrictions regarding the number of plants and the location where they are grown. Legally licensed dispensaries also sell marijuana to people over the age of 21, making pot more accessible than ever. However, it is important for people living in these states to still consider the physical and mental effects of marijuana use before deciding to smoke it themselves.

Chapter Three

MODERN MARIJUANA USE

According to the DEA, marijuana is grown illegally in all 50 states. Even in states where marijuana is legal, there are many restrictions on home growth, and the laws vary from state to state. For example, in Colorado, where recreational use is legal, the grower must be at least 21 years old; may only grow six plants, only three of which can be mature or flowering; may not grow them in an open space such as a backyard; and may not sell it to others, although giving away 1 ounce (28.3 g) or less for free to other adults is legal. In Washington, another state where recreational marijuana is legal, no one except licensed growers is allowed to cultivate these plants. Marijuana can most often be found growing in basements, where bright artificial lights are used to mimic the sunlight that is vital to the growth of all plant life. It can also be found in sprawling fields hidden deep in backwoods country and growing in places where authorities are unlikely to find it.

International Smuggling

Although police often find marijuana growing in America, the drug is also imported into the country by being smuggled across the border in a variety of ways. Marijuana is grown in Mexico and other Latin American countries, as well as Caribbean nations such as Jamaica. Thailand is also regarded as a major marijuana-producing country. These are places where the tropical climate and rich soil combine to make ideal conditions for the cultivation of the plant.

When it comes to growing marijuana, a tropical climate is not necessary, but it helps. Marijuana is a hardy and vigorous plant,

Grow rooms often do not have windows, but they use bright lights to imitate sunshine.

Border patrol officers use dogs to sniff out drugs in smugglers' cars.

capable of growing wherever there is soil, sun, and rain. Indeed, marijuana is grown in abundance in Canada, a country with a short growing season due to its cold climate. It is legal for medical use everywhere in the country, and Justin Trudeau, Canada's prime minister, has pledged to legalize it for recreational use in the near future.

The most common method smugglers use to bring marijuana into America is to drive it across the Mexican and Canadian borders. Each day, tens of thousands of cars and trucks drive through the many United States customs stations along the two borders. Border patrol agents inspect many vehicles, but there are simply not enough inspectors to look through each car and truck that stops at the border. However, Presidents Bush and Obama both increased the number of agents, taking it from 9,800 to about 21,444 between 2001 and 2011.

With more border patrol agents looking through cars and trucks at the borders, smugglers have been forced to resort to other means to bring drugs into the country. Boats and planes are used, certainly, but the National Drug Intelligence Center reports that cars and trucks are still the major method of bringing marijuana into the United States. According to the agency, if the smugglers decide not to chance a crossing at a border patrol station, they can easily employ an off-road vehicle to drive across the thousands of miles of open wilderness that are available along the Canadian and Mexican borders. A report by the agency said:

> The transportation of marijuana from foreign areas to the United States, as well as the transportation of foreign and domestic marijuana within the United States, occurs overwhelmingly by land. Transportation also occurs by sea and air; however, smugglers continue to exploit the breadth of the U.S. land borders with Mexico and Canada, transporting huge amounts of marijuana via official border checkpoints as well as countless unofficial crossing points.[25]

In recent years, marijuana smugglers have turned to other means to sneak the drug across the borders. Since 2001, when the border crackdown started, drug agents have uncovered more than 20 tunnels dug beneath the Mexican and Canadian borders. In early 2016, authorities uncovered a tunnel 0.5 mile (0.8 km) long, stretching from Tijuana, Mexico, to the town of Otay Mesa, California, just across the border. Inside the tunnel, police found several thousand pounds of marijuana and cocaine awaiting shipment. Six people were arrested on smuggling charges. Authorities say it is the longest, narrowest tunnel they have found so far in California.

Less Support for Cartels

One welcome effect of legalization in the United States has been the decline in the amount of marijuana being imported from Mexico. It is now safer and easier for people to get their weed, both legally and illegally, from growers in the United States. This removes some of the financial support for violent Mexican drug cartels, although these gangs still control the cocaine and heroin trades, as well as about one-third of the marijuana trade.

In some cases, the profits from marijuana sales are used to support political causes. In the South American country of Colombia, marijuana profits fund groups such as the Revolutionary Armed Forces of Colombia, the National Liberation Army, and the United Self-Defense Force. Each group requires large sums of money to buy arms for their insurgent rebels, who seek to topple the Colombian government.

Elsewhere, though, marijuana exports are managed by drug lords who harbor no revolutionary causes and are instead interested in nothing more than money. Before he died in a shootout with Mexican police in 1987, the drug lord Pablo Acosta headed an organization responsible for smuggling tons of marijuana into the United States—often hidden beneath shipments of cantaloupes trucked across the border. Another drug lord, Rafael Caro Quintero, presided over a marijuana plantation, known as the Buffalo, in the Mexican state of Chihuahua. The plantation covered 4.6 square miles (12 sq km) and employed approximately 12,000 farmworkers who were responsible for cultivating, cutting, packaging, and shipping the marijuana north to America. The plantation was shut down in 1985 after the murder of DEA agent Enrique Camarena, who discovered the operation. Caro Quintero was sentenced to 92 years in prison on murder charges.

Authorities eventually caught up with Acosta and Caro Quintero, and as marijuana becomes less profitable for cartels, many are concentrating more on cocaine and heroin. This means that marijuana users are less likely to be funding violent crime by buying pot, although it is still a possibility when that pot is obtained illegally. State regulations ensure that the weed being sold by registered dispensaries is ethically grown and distributed.

The Illegal Sale of Weed

In states where marijuana is still illegal, dealers obtain it from a smuggler or domestic supplier, or they grow it illegally themselves. They then sell it to friends or friends of friends. Typically, a dealer sells it by the ounce (28.3 g), which is enough marijuana to produce between 30 and 60 hand-rolled joints, depending on how much pot is rolled into each joint.

Dealers typically sell weed by the ounce. They weigh it before they sell it to make sure the amount is accurate.

THE COST OF INCARCERATION

Another benefit of legalization and decriminalization is that fewer people are going to jail for possession of the drug. This means the jails are less crowded and that fewer tax dollars are being used to pay for prisoners' upkeep. According to the news website Mic.com:

Let us work out some arithmetic based again on FBI statistics. In 2011, law enforcement personnel arrested a massive 12,408,899 individuals. Of these, 1,531,251, 12.3%, were for "drug abuse violations." 49.5% of these individuals were for crimes relating to marijuana. That is 757,969 people arrested for crimes dealing with marijuana. Knowing how many people were arrested in 2011 for marijuana related offenses, let us calculate the cost of this incarceration for taxpayers.

According to Urban Institute Justice Policy Center, the yearly cost for an inmate in a minimum security prison is $21,006. Let us use this figure because 56% of all inmates are housed in minimum security institutions. According to the U.S. Sentencing Commission, in 2010, the average prison sentence for inmates incarcerated for marijuana abuses is 36.8 months.

With 757,969 individuals incarcerated for marijuana abuse, at $21,006 a pop, that is $15,921,896,814 to keep these individuals imprisoned for one year. At this rate, over the course of 36.8 months, $44,765,690,442 would have to be coughed up by the American taxpayer to clothe, shelter, offer medical, dental and psychiatric care, maintain, transport, and educate these individuals and maintain facilities for them to live in. This— $44 billion over more than 30 years—is the grand cost of petty crime.[1]

---

1. Anthony Papastrat, "This Is How Much Marijuana Prohibition Costs You, the Taxpayer," Mic, July 18, 2013. mic.com/articles/54803/this-is-how-much-marijuana-prohibition-costs-you-the-taxpayer#.41TxXYla3.

The price of marijuana varies from city to city. It is also likely to vary day to day. Like most commodities, the price is based on the quality of the product, its availability, and what the consumer is willing to pay. In many cases, though, the price also depends on how vigilant the local police are in rounding up street dealers. If the police are running sweeps, which means dealers have to be on the lookout for undercover drug agents making buys, then the price is going to be higher.

Since legalization, the price of marijuana has fallen because it is more readily available and there is more competition among dispensaries and dealers. According to *Forbes* magazine, the national average for an ounce is $324. Oregon, where weed is legal both medically and recreationally, has the lowest price, at $204. The highest is North Dakota, at $387 per ounce.

Pot in Pop Culture

The people who are willing to pay those prices come from virtually every walk of life. Some are quite famous. In fact, the list of celebrity pot smokers is rather long. Occasionally, some have been arrested for possession of marijuana. Among them is actor Matthew McConaughey, who was arrested after police responded to his neighbors' noise complaints and found paraphernalia in his house. Singers Whitney Houston, James Brown, and David Lee Roth, as well as rappers Rick Ross and Wiz Khalifa, have been arrested on pot charges. Olympic swimmer Michael Phelps was not arrested when a photograph of him smoking weed surfaced in 2009, but he suffered repercussions to his career: USA Swimming suspended him for three months

Wiz Khalifa is one of many celebrities who have faced charges for possession of marijuana.

and one of his sponsors said it would not renew his contract. The rapper Dr. Dre has long professed a devotion to marijuana. One of his biggest records, *The Chronic*, included several rap songs that praised the use of pot. "Chronic" is a street term for a particularly potent strain of marijuana.

Another singer who has glorified marijuana is country singer Willie Nelson. The cover of his album *Countryman* featured green marijuana leaves—a design that prompted Wal-Mart to ban sales of the record in its stores. Nelson has never been secretive about his love for marijuana. In the late 1970s, he claimed to have smoked marijuana in the White House, where he was staying as a guest of President Jimmy Carter's family. In 1995, he was arrested in Texas when police found pot in his car. A judge later ruled that the search violated Nelson's rights, and the charges were dropped.

Nelson intended *Countryman* to pay tribute to reggae, the style of music popularized in Jamaica by the late singer Bob Marley. Before his death from brain cancer in 1981, Marley was a dedicated smoker of ganja, the Jamaican term for pot. The cover of Marley's best-selling album, *Catch a Fire*, featured a photograph of him smoking a spliff, which is a particularly fat marijuana cigarette. Peter Tosh, another reggae singer, released a hit single in 1976 titled "Legalize It," which called on the government to make marijuana a legal substance.

Then there is the story of Paul McCartney, the famous singer who was arrested in 1980 at a Japanese airport when customs inspectors found 0.5 pound (225 g) of pot hidden in his suitcase. McCartney spent 10 days in jail before he was released and kicked out of the country. At the time, McCartney was on a world tour with his band Wings, which he formed after leaving The Beatles. Angrily, McCartney declared he would never again play a concert in Japan. Years later, he recalled, "I was out in New York and I had all this really good grass. We were about to fly to Japan and I knew I wouldn't be able to get anything to smoke over there. This stuff was too good to flush down the toilet, so I thought I'd take it with me."[26]

McCartney says he has since given up marijuana, but while on a recent visit to Los Angeles he was approached by a group of teenagers who offered to share their pot with him. He said, "To me, it's a huge compliment that a bunch of kids think I might be up to smoke a bit of dope with them."[27]

Who Smokes?

When celebrities such as Paul McCartney, Willie Nelson, and Dr. Dre talk about their marijuana smoking habits, it makes national news. However, as statistics show, millions of other people in America smoke pot. Marijuana smokers can be found, for example, on many college campuses. In a profile of University of California at Santa Cruz students nicknamed Molly and Moppy, *Rolling Stone* reported:

> *There's always a little bit of surplus cash around for Molly and Moppy, because of Moppy's minor place on the great Northern California weed-distribution chain. He gets his herb from his friend Ben [not his real name] whose dad is part of a pot-growing collective in Humboldt County. Ben brings down about six pounds of pot a month, which he keeps in his closet in a safe the size of a gym locker. He pays his dad $3,000 per pound and generally makes $2,200 profit from selling it in quarter-pounds. Normally, when Moppy comes over to do a transaction, he and Ben sit with a bong, talking trash and truth, but last week Ben had a cold and didn't smoke for a few days—for the first time in nine years, in fact—and now he's trying to stay off it. Withdrawal is bringing him down. "I wasn't expecting to sell in Santa Cruz," says Ben, as Moppy hits the bong anyway. "I came to school with just a little personal sack of weed. But everyone in my dorm kept coming over because I was from Humboldt: 'You're from Humboldt! I know you have weed!'"[28]*

However, weed is not only available to college students. Monitoring the Future, the annual University of Michigan survey of drug use among middle school and high school students, reported in 2015 that 15 percent of American eighth-grade

MARIJUANA IN RELIGIOUS CEREMONIES

Several religions employ marijuana to help their members perform acts of worship. For example, during holidays, some Hindus consume bhang, which is a paste made from cannabis. This paste is often mixed with milk and spices to produce a drink or with sugar and ghee (clarified butter) to make a type of candy. They believe bhang helps them worship the Hindu god Shiva.

Hindus who found work as farm laborers in Jamaica during the 1800s introduced cannabis to the island. In the 1930s, the use of cannabis was embraced by a small Jamaican religious sect known as the Rastafarians, who believe marijuana opens their minds and helps them worship Haile Selassie, who became the king of Ethiopia in 1930 and whom Rastafarians believe to be a god. Today, it is estimated that there are some 1 million Rastafarians worldwide, with most living in Jamaica and other Caribbean nations.

The Rastafarians' devotion to marijuana, which they call ganja, has repeatedly caused them trouble. Rastafarians living in Jamaica, America, and elsewhere have been prosecuted on drug offenses and often made to serve prison sentences. However, as of 2015, Jamaica has decriminalized possession of small amounts of marijuana and legalized it for religious use. The United States has not yet legalized marijuana for this purpose.

Holi is an Indian holiday celebrating spring and color. It is the one time of year using marijuana, or bhang, is considered acceptable in India.

students said that they had smoked marijuana at least once in their lives. Meanwhile, on the other side of the spectrum, author Larry Sloman wrote about encountering an elderly couple, Abe and Lilyan, while researching his book *Reefer Madness* (which has nothing to do with the film of the same name). Abe and Lilyan, who live in the middle-class neighborhood of Bayside in Queens, New York, admitted to being longtime devotees of pot.

Lilyan said she had smoked marijuana as a teenager, then gave it up. However, when her own children reached their teenage years, Lilyan said she found their stash of marijuana in the home and tried smoking it again herself. She said: "I felt good. I felt that I wanted to talk to somebody, but there was nobody in the house to talk to. So I put on the record player and I started dancing and singing. I was having a great time. And that was it, my first time. I didn't realize till then that it was the same reefer that we smoked when we were kids."[29]

Another couple, Bill and Deb, are in their late 50s and have smoked since they were teenagers. They both enjoy smoking marijuana because they say it takes the edge off of their anxiety and makes them feel calmer. They consider this a health benefit and have no plans to stop smoking.

The Debate Over Medical Marijuana

Not all the marijuana that is either homegrown or smuggled into the country is used for recreational purposes. In fact, many people who smoke marijuana do not do it to get high from the drug, but rather to help ease the painful symptoms they suffer because of debilitating diseases. Indeed, some effects of the drug have been endorsed by health care professionals as acceptable treatments for pain and other ramifications of disease. For example, the dreamy, euphoric high that makes it hard for people to concentrate can also serve as an analgesic, meaning it is an effective painkiller. That can be an enormous benefit to cancer patients and others who suffer from long-term pain. Also, marijuana's propensity for making people hungry has surfaced as a treatment for the sufferers of acquired immunodeficiency syndrome, or AIDS, as well as people undergoing chemotherapy, which is the aggressive use of chemicals to kill cancer cells. In many cases, AIDS and chemo-therapy patients lose their appetites and suffer from malnutrition. By smoking marijuana, though, many of them regain the desire to eat.

For years, a significant debate has raged in American society over the rights of ill people to ease their suffering by consuming marijuana. The debate has reached the highest levels of govern-ment and the courts. Marijuana is now legal for medical purpos-es in 25 of the 50 states, but a significant faction continues to dispute this, convinced that the risks of marijuana use outweigh the benefits.

Chapter Four

MARIJUANA AS MEDICINE

Marijuana has been used as a medicine all around the world for thousands of years. In the United States, doctors recommended it to their patients right up until the Marihuana Tax Act of 1937 was passed. People used it to treat a variety of conditions, including nausea, insomnia, and migraines. This is one reason why so many people support the legalization movement: They say that it gives relief to sufferers of many different ailments. When the AIDS epidemic began in the 1980s, it was discovered that marijuana helped patients regain the appetite that AIDS took from them, helping them eat more so they would not suffer from malnutrition. This caused many gay people, who were affected by the AIDS epidemic in large numbers, and their friends and families to campaign for legalization.

After several studies were done by the American Medical Association (AMA), enough evidence was gathered to convince several states to legalize marijuana for medical use only. In those states, a doctor must prescribe marijuana, but they will often only do so after all other options have been exhausted. Laws vary from state to state regarding whether patients are allowed to have a smokable or non-smokable supply, as well as whether or not they are allowed to grow their own plants.

As pot continues to gain mainstream popularity, more studies will be conducted and new research will continue to emerge. What we know about marijuana right now could very well be proven wrong in a few years' time. However, the vast majority of medical marijuana users believe that the benefits they receive from using the drug far outweigh any ill effects they may experience.

THE FIRST MEDICAL MARIJUANA PROGRAM

Federal prosecutors have ordered the arrests of medical marijuana growers, but at one time, the government believed marijuana did have promise as a drug that could treat pain and other symptoms of disease. In 1976, the United States Food and Drug Administration established the experimental Compassionate Investigational New Drug program. The program provided marijuana cigarettes to a handful of patients to gauge their reactions to the drug.

The first patient admitted under the program was a glaucoma sufferer. The disease causes a painful pressure on the eyes, and studies have shown that marijuana helps ease the pain. By 1992, the program was flooded with applicants who wished to participate. Rather than expand the program, the administration of President George H. W. Bush elected to close it to new applicants, although the dozen or so patients already in the program continued to receive their government-grown pot, which is cultivated in a closely guarded field at the University of Mississippi. By 2012, just four patients were still part of the program. One of them is George McMahon, a Frankton, Texas, man who suffers from nail-patella syndrome, a rare deformity of the bones.

McMahon has traveled the country, speaking in favor of legalization of medical marijuana. He said, "According to the federal laws of this free nation, sick patients who use marijuana to ease their pain are labeled common criminals. In the meantime, people are dying. And I am dedicated to bring their plight to the attention of those who could change it."[1]

1. George McMahon and Christopher Largen, *Prescription Pot: A Leading Advocate's Heroic Battle to Legalize Medical Marijuana*. Far Hills, NJ: New Horizon, 2003, p. 20.

Ryan G. lives in New York State, where medical marijuana is legal. Patients in New York are allowed to possess a 30-day supply of non-smokable marijuana and are not allowed to cultivate their own plants. Ryan feels that since he has started using cannabis oil, his quality of life has significantly improved.

When I turned 16, I was on my way to my first job, and I threw up all over my shoes. From that point forward, that's just the way it was. I was sick all the time. Years later, I also developed a pain that I can only describe as [feeling like] shards of glass in my stomach, which was at its worst first thing in the morning. I was diagnosed with mitochondrial disorder, a neurological disorder with no cure that cripples many of the people diagnosed with it. Nothing my doctor prescribed for the nausea or the pain worked. I started taking medical cannabis on a Monday. By Tuesday morning, both the nausea and the stabbing pains were gone. I could wake up in the morning without feeling thrashed. I feel like I got a small portion of my life back.[30]

The public debate over the benefits of medical marijuana set the stage for a legal challenge that would eventually be decided by the U.S. Supreme Court. On one side, the U.S. Justice Department fought to uphold the Controlled Substances Act, which for more than three decades, held that marijuana had no useful medical purpose. On the other side stood the sufferers of AIDS, cancer, and other painful diseases, who felt that they should have access to the only drug that provides them with relief and that they should not have to break the law to use it.

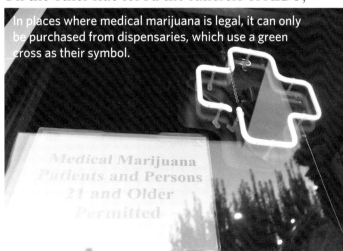

In places where medical marijuana is legal, it can only be purchased from dispensaries, which use a green cross as their symbol.

California Paves the Way

California's large gay population has been a driving force behind the legalization movement. San Francisco, in particular, had been hit hard during the AIDS epidemic. In 1991, gay activists organized the drive to slate Proposition P on the ballot in San Francisco. The ballot question asked voters whether California should legalize medical marijuana. The measure passed with 80 percent of the vote. Since Proposition P was limited to the city of San Francisco, it had no effect on California's state laws banning marijuana use; it merely proved to government officials that the majority of San Francisco citizens supported statewide legalization.

Still, the activists were encouraged by the response from San Francisco voters, and they urged the city's board of supervisors to adopt a resolution decriminalizing medical marijuana. The supervisors agreed, passing a resolution that stated, "San Francisco Police and the District Attorney will place as its lowest priority enforcement of marijuana laws that interfere with the medical application of this valued herb."[31]

One of the leaders of the California legalization movement was Dennis Peron, a gay San Francisco man whose partner, Jonathan West, died from AIDS. Peron watched how the disease robbed West of his strength and appetite, and also how cannabis eased his suffering. Following West's death, Peron established a farm near the town of Williams, deep in the Northern California countryside. Peron grows pot on the farm exclusively for medical purposes. He opposes the movement to legalize it for recreational use. "All use is medical," he says. "If you're smoking recreationally, just to get high, first I think you're stupid, and second, I don't have any time for you."[32]

Treating Debilitating Diseases

Medical marijuana activists were not satisfied with their victory in San Francisco. Following adoption of Proposition P, Peron and other activists organized a statewide movement to convince the California Assembly that medical marijuana should be legalized. In 1996, they succeeded in slating a statewide ballot question asking voters to approve Proposition 215, also known as the California Compassionate Use Act, legalizing the use of marijuana by anyone who obtains the recommendation of a physician for treatment of "cancer, anorexia, AIDS, chronic fatigue, spasticity, glaucoma, arthritis, migraine headaches, or any other illness for which marijuana provides relief."[33]

Voters approved the measure, making California the first state to legalize medical marijuana. Within a few years, nine more states—Alaska, Arizona, Colorado, Hawaii, Maine, Montana, Nevada, Oregon, and Washington—had enacted similar laws. Many other states only decriminalized marijuana at first, then legalized it for medical use after several more years had passed. Thus far, only four states—Alaska, Colorado, Oregon, and Washington—have legalized it for recreational purposes.

Legislatures in those states reacted to the will of their voters, but also to the mounting scientific evidence that suggests marijuana does possess medical qualities. In 2001, the AMA issued a report summarizing the findings of a number of scientific studies. The AMA found, for example, that marijuana's propensity for making its users hungry could be an enormous benefit to AIDS sufferers, who are often made nauseated by the disease as well as the harsh drugs used to treat the ailment. Likewise, the AMA found cancer patients forced to endure chemotherapy could also benefit from consuming marijuana. Chemotherapy can be an effective treatment, but when patients' bodies are bombarded by the chemicals, they often grow ill and nauseated and have difficulty keeping their food down.

Multiple sclerosis patients were also found to benefit from consuming cannabis. These patients suffer from spasticity, meaning their muscles grow rigid. Cannabis relaxes their muscles and gives them freedom of movement, the AMA found.

The AMA also found that glaucoma patients could get relief from cannabis. Marijuana was found to ease the pressure suffered by glaucoma patients. However, in this case, the AMA cautioned that marijuana may not be the right medicine for many glaucoma sufferers. Since many glaucoma patients are elderly, the association said, caution should be urged in the use of mari-

Sufferers of many different ailments have found relief through medical marijuana.

juana because the drug can also cause the pulse to race, a potentially fatal side effect for elderly users. Additionally, according to *Scientific American* magazine, "several studies have found that smoking marijuana ... [relieves] glaucoma-related discomfort for about three to four hours. Yet a number of pharmaceutical drugs have been shown to be more effective and longer lasting than medical marijuana."[34]

Finally, the AMA concluded that the single most important use of medical marijuana is to treat pain. For years, medical researchers have struggled to develop effective analgesics, but many highly effective drugs can be prescribed today for severe pain. In most cases, those treatments are drawn from the class of drugs known as opioids, which can be highly addictive. In fact, the illegal and addictive drug heroin is an opioid. While marijuana does have addictive qualities, the AMA suggested that marijuana may be far less addictive than most opioids. The association recommended further study into the use of marijuana as a pain reliever.

Although all of these findings prompted legal change, new studies are being performed all the time, and they may well overturn these results at some point in the future. *Scientific American* magazine cautions that, "until recently, the drug's illegal status impeded rigorous study of its effectiveness."[35] Pharmaceutical research in other areas is also ongoing, so new drugs may make marijuana obsolete as a remedy.

Many people claim that marijuana is better than medicines created in a lab because it is natural. However, opium comes from poppies, shown here. Scientific studies are important because "natural" does not always mean "safe," and "man-made" does not always mean "dangerous."

Non-Smokable Marijuana

Medical marijuana advocates embraced the AMA report when it was released, declaring that an influential and respected national organization had now recognized the validity of medical marijuana. Yet the concept of legalizing pot for medical purposes still has its critics. Sheryl Massaro, a spokesperson for NIDA, said that legalizing marijuana for medical reasons could suggest to people that using pot for recreational purposes is acceptable and harmless. "Seeming to legalize marijuana for anything would give young people the wrong impression," she said. "That doesn't even seem to enter the minds of a lot of people who are promoting it for medical use."[36] Medical College of Virginia pharmacology professor Billy R. Martin insisted that there are many legitimate drugs that can provide the same benefits as cannabis. In addition to the well-known painkillers, Martin said, pharmaceutical companies have recently developed drugs to counter the nausea brought on by AIDS and chemotherapy. "There are better drugs out there,"[37] he said.

In order to combat these concerns, as well as reduce the negative effects smoking has on the lungs, a drug called Marinol was developed in the 1980s. It incorporates THC into a pill form. Marinol was the forerunner of the modern medical marijuana movement. It is still sometimes prescribed, but other forms of non-smokable marijuana have since been developed and are more widely used. Ryan G. used to smoke, but now he prefers the cannabis oil he is prescribed:

Taking cannabis in oil form lasts twice as long as smoking it. I can now go to and stay at parties longer. I can attend sporting events again without having to worry about what happens when the effects wear off. I lost the smoker's cough I had obtained. [Also], the quality of medical, legal cannabis oil is far beyond what most people would find [in illegal, smokable form]. With illegal pot, there are no quality checks. It isn't regulated. There's no Better Business Bureau you can report your drug dealer to. There are no rules, and if someone [cheats you], you're left with no legal recourse. I felt like a criminal for just taking the medication I needed. I had to hide it from my friends [when I smoked illegally]. Now, I can take some cannabis oil at home, have my stomach feel pretty good for six hours (instead of two to four if I had smoked), and I can now be discreet when medicating myself without leaving smoke and a stink.[38]

A doctor may prescribe cannabis oil for people who want pain relief but do not want to get high.

Critics believe Marinol and other pill-like methods have their shortcomings and are far less effective than marijuana. For example, since they enter the blood through the stomach lining, pills take far more time to work. Asking an AIDS or cancer patient to spend a few more minutes waiting for relief may not seem like much to ask, but the patient who is enduring chronic nausea or gut-wrenching vomiting may disagree. University of Arizona pharmacology professor Paul Consroe said another important difference between Marinol and pot is that a medical marijuana smoker needs to smoke only enough of the drug to find relief, whereas a Marinol user gets the full jolt of whatever is in the pill. He said, "With smoked marijuana, patients get immediate relief, whereas with the oral drug they get a delayed, big rush of unpleasantness. When they take a small dose [of Marinol] it doesn't work."[39] One method that addresses these problems is to administer marijuana as a tincture—extracting the active compounds into a liquid form and applying it under the tongue. In this way, proponents claim, "tinctures enter the bloodstream immediately, allowing for fast-acting effects and better dose control."[40]

Critics also oppose medical marijuana because, even if it benefits patients, it has the side effect of getting them stoned or high, which makes them unable to function in everyday life, particularly at work or school. These non-smokable methods solve that problem because they are so low in THC that they do not get the user high. However, no form of marijuana should be used without being prescribed by a doctor. Not only is it illegal to do so, there is no way of knowing what kinds of side effects may occur or whether it will interact with other medicines.

States vs. the Federal Government

In 2002, United States attorney general John Ashcroft declared that he would crack down on medical marijuana growers. Ashcroft insisted that the 1970 federal Controlled Substances Act took precedence over the state laws that permitted marijuana for medical purposes, meaning that whatever the laws of California, Oregon, and the other states permitted, growing, selling, and using marijuana for medical purposes is illegal under federal law. He directed the DEA to investigate and arrest medical marijuana growers.

The DEA responded that year by raiding the home of Diane Monson, who grew marijuana in her backyard garden in Oroville, California. Monson started smoking pot to ease her own chronic back pain. In the raid on Monson's garden, the DEA seized six plants. Monson fought back, asking the courts to prohibit the Justice Department from prosecuting the growers and users of medical marijuana. Monson enlisted Angel Raich, an outspoken proponent of legalization, as an ally. The two women filed a lawsuit against the Justice Department, arguing that the federal government could not enforce the Controlled Substances Act in states that had adopted medical marijuana laws.

A federal judge rejected the women's claim and refused to bar the Justice Department from enforcing the Controlled Substances Act on medical marijuana growers, but in 2003, an appeals court sided with Monson and Raich. The appeals court said that Congress, which enacted the Controlled Substances Act, exceeded its authority by prohibiting use of a medically advantageous drug. At that point, the Justice Department appealed the case to the U.S. Supreme Court. Arguments were held before the court in November 2004; seven months later, the court issued its opinion. The court ruled that the federal government does have the power under the 1970 law to prosecute growers and users of medical marijuana, despite what state laws may allow. In recent years, the federal government has mostly turned its attention to other matters, but unless marijuana is legalized at the federal level, the government could focus on this issue again at any time.

MARIJUANA FOR MENTAL ILLNESSES?

Few tests have been done on the effectiveness of marijuana's physical health benefits, and even fewer have been done on its purported mental health benefits. However, people have used it illegally for years to treat the symptoms of conditions such as autism, anxiety, depression, obsessive-compulsive disorder (OCD), attention deficit/hyperactivity disorder (ADHD), Alzheimer's disease, insomnia, and more. Joe L. has ADHD and agrees that being stoned makes him feel less hyperactive, but he says it does not help improve his concentration and, in fact, makes it worse.

Recently, a new strain of marijuana was bred in Israel that may give relief from these disorders without getting the user high or stoned. The breed does not contain THC, but it does contain cannabidiol (CBD). Researchers believe that CBD is the compound responsible for producing weed's calming effects, while THC can cause hallucinations, paranoia, and increased appetite (known as the "munchies"). According to *TIME* magazine, "A preliminary trial of CBD for the treatment of people with schizophrenia found that it was as effective as a standard antipsychotic drug—with none of the movement disorders, mood issues, or weight gain linked to that class of medications. CBD also seems to protect brain cells from damage, so much so that it is currently being studied as a way to stop the progression of the movement disorder Huntington's disease, which is caused by degeneration of nerve cells in certain parts of the brain."[1] This kind of marijuana may prove to be a safer way to treat mental and neurological disorders, but much more study is needed before it can be prescribed this way.

1. Maia Szalavitz, "A New Marijuana Plant Without the High? It Could Be Good Medicine," *TIME*, June 4, 2012. healthland.time.com/2012/06/04/a-new-marijuana-plant-without-the-high-it-could-be-good-medicine/.

Why Pot Is Still Illegal

In writing the Supreme Court's opinion, Justice John Paul Stevens said it is clear that AIDS and cancer victims and other sufferers of debilitating diseases have valid reasons for wanting to use medical marijuana. Stevens said he was moved by the afflictions that plagued Raich and Monson. Nevertheless, Stevens said, it is evident that the amount of marijuana grown in the United States and imported from other countries is far in excess of what medical marijuana users require. Clearly, Stevens said, if the court permitted the production of medical marijuana, it would not take long for the pot to wind up in the wrong hands. "The likelihood that all such production … will precisely match the patients' needs … seems remote, whereas the danger that excesses will satisfy some of the admittedly enormous demand for recreational use seems obvious,"[41] he said.

Advocates for medical marijuana were shocked and saddened by the Supreme Court decision. Angel Raich vowed to keep using cannabis. "It is absolutely cruel that the federal government does not allow us the right to use this medicine," Raich said. "It is not easy for patients that really need this medicine … to have to fight for our lives on this kind of level."[42]

A Long Way to Go

Although medical marijuana is legal in half of the United States and Washington, D.C., there are still restrictions on its use that can make it very difficult for someone to try to get a prescription. The list of conditions eligible for medical marijuana is generally limited only to life-threatening or extremely painful diseases. In New York State, for example, a patient must have "a specific severe, debilitating, or life threatening condition that is accompanied by an associated or complicating condition."[43] For example, someone must have cancer and severe nausea, or epilepsy and muscle spasms. Insomnia, depression, glaucoma, and other less severe conditions are not recognized as legitimate reasons for a marijuana prescription. As with all other marijuana laws, these restrictions vary by state. California, for instance, has a much more liberal policy.

Angel Raich has been an outspoken advocate for marijuana legalization.

Even people who have one of the conditions on the list may encounter difficulties, Ryan G. said:

The hardest part is finding a doctor. Of the over 7,000 doctors in New York State, only about 600 of them are registered to prescribe marijuana right now. My primary care physician didn't know anyone who could prescribe it to me; neither did my pain management specialist. I had to do all the work of researching, which is extremely hard because New York State will only release a list of registered doctors to other doctors; it's not open to the public. Once you do get a prescription, for some people in New York State, it's a five-hour drive to the nearest dispensary.[44]

These facts prove that although medical marijuana has been legalized, there is still a long way to go to provide universal relief for sufferers. However, with legalization steadily growing at the state level, it may only be a matter of time before the federal government gives up the battle.

Chapter Five

THE BATTLE FOR LEGALIZATION

Ever since marijuana was first outlawed, people have been campaigning to have that decision overturned. In addition to the health and recreational reasons, proponents of legalization are not in favor of the strict penalties that can be enacted on people who are caught with marijuana. In states where it is decriminalized, only a first-time offender is let off with a slap on the wrist. Federal mandatory minimum laws are in place, meaning that a person who breaks that particular law must serve a minimum amount of time in jail and may indeed serve more time. Judges have no ability to sentence less time for crimes that have a mandatory minimum penalty attached, but they can sentence more or enact a fine as well as a jail sentence. For possession, the sentence is no less than 15 days in jail for a second offense and no less than 90 days for any subsequent offense, no matter how small an amount of pot the person is caught with. Many people believe these are unreasonably harsh penalties for a nonviolent crime.

The core objection of the legalization movement is that people should not be punished by the government for doing something that does not harm anyone except the user. People take risks every day, but most of these are not illegal unless they directly harm another person. For example, alcohol and tobacco are both legal even though they sometimes kill their users. However, drunk driving is not legal because it has the potential to kill or seriously injure innocent people, and there are laws regarding how close someone can stand to a building when he or she is smoking to prevent non-smokers from inadvertently

Federal Trafficking Penalties for Marijuana, Hashish and Hashish Oil, Schedule I Substances

Marijuana
1,000 kilograms or more marijuana mixture or 1,000 or more marijuana plants

First Offense: Not less than 10 years or more than life. If death or serious bodily injury, not less than 20 years or more than life. Fine not more than $10 million if an individual, $50 million if other than an individual.

Second Offense: Not less than 20 years or more than life. If death or serious bodily injury, life imprisonment. Fine not more than $20 million if an individual, $75 million if other than an individual.

Marijuana
100 to 999 kilograms marijuana mixture or 50 to 99 marijuana plants

First Offense: Not less than 5 years or more than 40 years. If death or serious bodily injury, not less than 20 years or more than life. Fine not more than $5 million if an individual, $25 million if other than an individual.

Second Offense: Not less than 10 years or more than life. If death or serious bodily injury, life imprisonment. Fine not more than $8 million if an individual, $50 million if other than an individual.

Marijuana
50 to 99 kilograms marijuana mixture or 100 to 999 marijuana plants

Hashish
more than 10 kilograms

Hashish Oil
more than 1 kilogram

First Offense: Not more than 20 years. If death or serious bodily injury, not less than 20 years or more than life. Fine $1 million if an individual, $5 million if other than an individual.

Second Offense: Not more than 30 years. If death or serious bodily injury, life imprisonment. Fine $2 million if an individual, $10 million if other than an individual.

Marijuana
less than 50 kilograms marijuana (but does not include 50 or more marijuana plants regardless of weight)

1 to 49 marijuana plants

Hashish
more than 10 kilograms

Hashish Oil
more than 1 kilogram

First Offense: Not more than 5 years. Fine not more than $250,000, or $1 million if other than an individual.

Second Offense: Not more than 10 years. Fine not more than $500,000, or $2 million if other than an individual.

These are the official penalties for trafficking, or dealing, marijuana, according to the DEA, which measures marijuana in kilograms.

inhaling secondhand smoke. R. Keith Stroup, the former executive director of NORML, said:

> It is time we adopted a marijuana policy that reflects a distinction between use and abuse, and reflects the importance most Americans place on the right of the individual to be free from the overreaching power of government. Most would agree that the government has no business knowing what books we read, the subject of our telephone conversations, or how we conduct ourselves in the bedroom. Similarly, whether one smokes marijuana or drinks alcohol to relax is simply not an appropriate area of concern for the government.[45]

Benefits of Legalization

Opinion polls show that a significant segment of the public is in agreement with Stroup. In 2015, a study conducted by the Pew Research Center found that 53 percent of Americans believe marijuana should be legal, and that 36 percent of those feel "that marijuana is no worse than other drugs—with many explicitly mentioning that they think it is no more dangerous than alcohol or cigarettes."[46] The truth of this claim is difficult to determine because of differences in the behavior of the users. Both marijuana and alcohol can have negative health effects if they are heavily used, although it has been proven that a person can die from drinking too much alcohol at one time, but not from smoking too much weed at one time. Many of the same chemicals are present in both cigarettes and joints, but marijuana users tend to smoke much less than cigarette users. Ultimately, more research is needed to determine whether any of these substances is more harmful than the others.

Regulating the distribution of marijuana has been recommended by some political leaders, who suggest that government control over marijuana is one way to keep the gangs and drug lords out of the business. They point out that once alcohol was made illegal, the beer and liquor business was taken over by gangsters. When Prohibition was repealed, the gangsters were driven out of the business, and legal brewers and distillers took over. Indeed, the same has proven true in marijuana legalization. The amount of weed being illegally imported from Mexico has drastically decreased in the last several years now that it is legal to grow it in parts of the United States, and people are more likely to buy it from a licensed dispensary than from a dealer.

Legal marijuana is inspected to make sure it has no mold or bugs on it before it is sold. Illegal marijuana is not.

Government regulation could also help ensure the purity of marijuana. Pot that is not inspected may be carrying bacteria that could spread disease. If pot becomes legal nationally, federal agencies such as the Food and Drug Administration and the Department of Agriculture would be responsible for inspecting the crop and setting standards that would have to be followed for production. Also, U.S. border patrol agents would inspect marijuana as it arrives at the borders. Right now, of course, no illegal pot is inspected, and customers do not always know what they are inhaling. Scientific studies of marijuana plants have shown that they are sometimes contaminated with mold, *E. coli*, or pesticides. For this reason, "Heather Miller Coyle, a forensic botanist and associate professor at the [University of New Haven] ... began developing a new process to detect contaminants in marijuana through DNA profiling and analysis. The aim is to be able to identify potentially harmful substances through a testing method that could make the analysis easier and quicker for labs across the country in the developing industry of marijuana quality control testing."[47]

When Prohibition was repealed in 1933, Congress quickly enacted a tax on alcohol that President Franklin Roosevelt used to finance the antipoverty programs of his New Deal that helped rescue Americans from the Great Depression. Since then, consumers of beer, wine, and liquor have continued to pay heavy taxes on the beverages. Proponents of legalizing marijuana suggest that if the government regulates the marijuana business, billions of dollars in new tax revenue could be raised. Most Americans would benefit because the other taxes they pay would be reduced. This has already happened in states where marijuana is legal recreationally. In the first year of legalization, Colorado sold $996,184,788 worth of pot and collected more than $135 million in taxes, much of which it intends to use for its schools. *Forbes* stated, "To put that in perspective, that's approximately one percent of the total annual budgets for New Mexico, Indiana, or Kansas."[48]

THE NATIONAL ORGANIZATION FOR THE REFORM OF MARIJUANA LAWS (NORML)

NORML was founded in 1970 by R. Keith Stroup, a young lawyer who had worked for the United States Commission on Product Safety, which was established to protect consumers from dangerous or faulty products. Stroup started using marijuana as a college student. While working as a consumer advocate, he conceived of the idea of an organization to speak up for the rights of marijuana consumers.

The organization initially had some success. In 1972, the National Commission on Marijuana, which had been appointed by President Richard Nixon, recommended that people who possess less than an ounce (28.3 g) of the drug should not be prosecuted. NORML brought the report to the attention of state legislatures, and due to NORML's efforts, five states—Alaska, California, Colorado, Maine, and Ohio—removed criminal penalties for possession of small amounts of the drug. According to the group's website, "NORML's mission is to move public opinion sufficiently to legalize the responsible use of marijuana by adults, and to serve as an advocate for consumers to assure they have access to high quality marijuana that is safe, convenient, and affordable."[1]

1. NORML.org, "About NORML." norml.org/about.

International Attitudes Toward Marijuana

In many other countries, people are given more freedom. The trend started in Europe in 1990, when drug abuse experts from four European cities—Amsterdam in the Netherlands, Frankfurt and Hamburg in Germany, and Zurich in Switzerland—met in Frankfurt to discuss ways of fighting addiction. They concluded that the zeal to arrest, prosecute, and imprison drug offenders had not worked. The group of drug experts, who formed the organization European Cities on Drug Policy, found that most drug users are not criminals, and throwing them in jail exposes them to real criminals, making it more likely they would break laws when they are released from prison. The representatives at the Frankfurt conference suggested that it may be wiser to let people use soft drugs, such as pot and hallucinogenic mushrooms, legally but to conduct public campaigns advising them of the risks and offering them programs to beat their addictions—much the same way alcohol and tobacco use is treated worldwide. However, they decided not to legalize hard drugs such as cocaine or heroin. They issued the Frankfurt Resolution, which states:

> Drug using is for the majority of users a temporary part of their biography, which can be overcome within the process of maturing out of addiction. Drug policy may not render this process more difficult, but it must support this process ... A drug policy fighting against addiction exclusively with the criminal law and the compulsion to abstinence and offering abstinence only has failed ... Criminalization is a counterpart to drug aid and drug therapy and is a burden for police and justice they cannot carry ... The aid for drug users must no longer be threatened by criminal law ... It is necessary to lay stress on harm reduction and repressive forms of intervention must be reduced to the absolute necessary minimum.[49]

Lawmakers in many European countries have adopted the spirit of the Frankfurt Resolution, particularly when it applies to marijuana use. The nations of Germany, Belgium, Denmark, Greece, Ireland, Holland, Portugal, Spain, and England have decriminalized marijuana, but they have not legalized its sale. Marijuana use in Italy remains a crime, but no penalty is assessed on the defendant. However, trafficking in drugs in those countries as well as others remains a crime; France, Greece, and Italy retain the stiffest laws, with sentences of up to 20 years for major traffickers.

As for the individual pot smoker, though, personal use in those European countries is treated as simply something that some people do. The Netherlands is regarded as having the most

Baked goods containing marijuana can be legally purchased at coffeeshops in Amsterdam.

liberal pot laws in Europe. In the city of Amsterdam, use of marijuana and hashish in public coffeehouses is permitted, although it cannot be used on the streets. Author Brian Preston describes his experience in Amsterdam while researching his book, *Pot Planet: Adventures in Global Marijuana Culture*:

> *Buying and smoking good pot in the coffee shops of Amsterdam, you can get high in comfort, stumble into the street, and ask a cop for directions. I said, "Excuse me" to get the attention of a cop one time, and he smiled back and said, "You are excused." I knew at that moment I reeked of weed, and I knew what an American activist had meant when he told me that sometimes in Amsterdam he felt like hugging the police.*[50]

However, has it worked? Have the European countries that abide by the spirit of the Frankfurt Resolution seen their addiction rates decline, or has much of Europe simply turned into a safe harbor for stoners? There is dispute over the success of the Frankfurt Resolution. *The Huffington Post* reports that some Dutch citizens have complained about the legalization of marijuana, leading the government to reduce the number of legal coffeeshops in the country. France and Germany have also complained; they share borders with the Netherlands and have seen an increase in the number of their citizens bringing pot into their countries, even though this is illegal. Some border towns tried to solve this problem by creating a registry for weed users, but "the independent-minded Dutch (especially young people), don't want to be registered as pot users, so they are buying it on the street—which is rekindling the black market, and will likely translate to more violence, turf wars, and hard drugs being sold."[51]

These problems aside, legalization has largely worked well for the Netherlands. Fewer Dutch use pot than Americans because it is treated as a mundane thing. By viewing marijuana as they do alcohol, the Dutch have turned the problem from a criminal issue into a health issue.

4/20: National Pot Day

Each April 20, thousands of people come together to celebrate marijuana. The tradition has its roots in San Rafael, California, where, starting in 1971, a group of high school students met each day at 4:20 p.m. to smoke marijuana. From there, it became a way for college students to show their support for legalization. Eventually, the tradition spread, and April 20—4/20 on the calendar—was set aside as an unofficial holiday to pay tribute to marijuana and rally for liberalization of marijuana laws. Yet even after legalization in states such as Washington and Oregon, the 4/20 rallies continue. They have lost much of their political association and have become simply a celebration where pot smokers can gather together and indulge in a pastime they enjoy.

For the most part, college officials frown on the events because, along with the demonstrating and speechmaking, there is always a copious amount of marijuana smoked by the people gathered. In 2005, 1,000 students gathered for a 4/20 event on the campus of the University of Colorado in Boulder, despite rainy conditions. "If it wasn't raining, this place would be even more packed,"[52] said Mason Tvert, director of the marijuana advocacy group Safer Alternatives for Enjoyable Recreation.

THE HEMP MARKET

Hemp is a form of cannabis, but it contains so little THC that getting high from it is impossible. Nevertheless, hemp was outlawed along with all other forms of marijuana in 1970 when the Controlled Substances Act said that marijuana has no legal purpose. Any hemp used for manufacturing in the United States has, until recently, been imported from other countries. However, in 2014, President Barack Obama exempted hemp from that law, making it legal to grow in the United States again.

The seeds and stalks of the hemp plant have many uses. For example, hemp oil extracted from the seed can be a component in fuel, lubricants, ink, varnish, paint, and cosmetics. The various parts of the stalk can create mulch, fiberboard, insulation, rope, clothes, cardboard, and ethanol. It is a sustainable crop that requires less water to grow than other crops, such as wheat, and can be used to purify soil, causing other crops to have fewer impurities.

The legalization of hemp is expected to have a major positive impact on the American economy and on the personal incomes of American farmers. Canadian farmers, who can legally grow hemp, made about $250 per acre in 2013—compared to North Dakota in 2014, which netted only $71 per acre for soy, one of its main crops. For farmers who are struggling to make ends meet, hemp could be the answer to their problems.

Hemp can be made into many products, including rope.

PRESIDENTS WHO SMOKED

In 1992, as Bill Clinton campaigned for the presidency, reports surfaced that he had experimented with marijuana while attending Oxford University in England. Clinton was forced to admit his marijuana use, although he acknowledged only a brief episode with the drug and even claimed not to have inhaled the smoke. The public doubted that story but did not hold it against him. He was elected president in 1992 and reelected four years later.

In 2000, as he campaigned for the presidency, George W. Bush acknowledged his own substance abuse problems, although he admitted publicly only to a prior drinking problem. In 2005, author Doug Wead reported in his book, *The Raising of a President*, that Bush had smoked marijuana but refused to answer questions from reporters about his use of the substance. "I wouldn't answer the marijuana questions," Bush told Wead. "You know why? Because I don't want some little kid doing what I tried."[1]

Barack Obama is one of several presidents who have admitted to trying marijuana.

In 2006, when he was running for his first term, reporters asked Barack Obama about passages from his book *Dreams from My Father* in which he said he had smoked pot as a young adult. Obama was direct and open about it, saying that he was not trying to condone pot smoking, but rather was documenting his years as a confused teenager.

Other politicians have admitted to smoking pot as well, including Bernie Sanders, Sarah Palin, and Arnold Schwarzenegger, the former governor of California.

1. Quoted in Doug Wead, *The Raising of a President: The Mothers and Fathers of Our Nation's Leaders.* New York, NY: Atria Books, 2005.

Racism in Drug Arrests

Typically, the DEA, the Federal Bureau of Investigation (FBI), and other federal law enforcement agencies do not target individual users of pot. Rather, federal agencies go after big-time drug lords. Still, penalties for simple possession are on the books, and individuals can be prosecuted in federal courts.

The 1986 mandatory minimum law was passed following the death of Len Bias, a college basketball star who celebrated his selection in the National Basketball Association draft by going to a party and ingesting a fatal dose of cocaine. The nation was shocked by the death of Bias. Responding to intense public pressure, federal lawmakers felt compelled to come down hard on all drug offenders. Much to the dismay of legalization advocates, Congress included marijuana users on the list of drug offenders who could be prosecuted under the law.

Legalization advocates insist that the 1986 law, as well as the many state laws that include jail sentences for offenders, has resulted in a tremendous number of people serving prison terms—both short and long—for marijuana offenses. However, despite equal usage among the races, black and Latino people are disproportionately arrested for this crime, while white people are more likely to get away with a fine or no penalty at all. The American Civil Liberties Union (ACLU) issued a report in 2013 showing that depending on the state, blacks are between

A study by the ACLU found that racism plays a large part in who is charged for possession of marijuana.

1.6 and 8.3 times more likely to be arrested than whites for possession. Decriminalization has caused the total number of arrests to fall, but not the racial inequality—blacks are still more likely than whites to be arrested for the same crime.

There are many complex reasons for this bias. One is that police tend to concentrate their patrols in low-income areas, where more black people are likely to live. Black people who are stopped by the police on the street or in a car may be asked to empty their pockets, regardless of whether they were doing anything illegal at the time. If they happen to have marijuana in their possession, they will likely be arrested and charged. In contrast, the police rarely search white or wealthy people. Teenagers are also targeted more often than adults.

A major reason why police do this is that for them, it is easy work that is low risk and high reward. Most teens who possess marijuana are not dangerous, but by a strictly legal definition, they are criminals, so the police are justified in arresting them. This may earn the police officers recognition at work and sometimes extra money without the worry of putting themselves at personal risk, as they would be if they were arresting someone for possession of an illegal firearm or an adult who might fight them. Many police departments judge officers' performance on the number of arrests made, which gives them an incentive to go after several easy targets rather than one or two difficult ones.

Unfortunately, there is no easy solution to the problem of racially disparate, or unequal, arrests. Legalizing marijuana would go a long way, but even that may not completely fix it, as people can still be arrested for things such as growing more plants than they are permitted or possessing more than the legally allowed amount. A massive overhaul of the way police departments function and the way our society views race is the only answer.

The Future of Marijuana

Supporters of marijuana for both recreation and medicine hope that states will continue to legalize pot, prompting the federal government to pass a sweeping resolution. Many states have already decriminalized pot or legalized it for medical purposes, but these laws vary from state to state and are often confusing. For example, it is decriminalized in New York State, but up until 2014, police were charging people caught in their homes with a fine, while those caught in a public space were charged with a misdemeanor. Those in favor of legalization point to the time and money police will save if they do not have to arrest individuals who possess small amounts of marijuana for personal use. They also state that marijuana is equally or even less harmful than alcohol and tobacco, and that the government has no business banning these items because it infringes on citizens' right to choose.

Although the legalization movement is gaining steam, slightly less than half of Americans still oppose it completely. Most are not in favor of legalizing medical marijuana because they worry that this is a slippery slope toward recreational legalization. Others claim that the health benefits are exaggerated or even fictionalized. Opponents feel that marijuana is a dangerous, addictive drug with the potential to ruin lives and lead people to use harder drugs such as cocaine and heroin.

The biggest roadblock to legalization thus far has been the absence of conclusive studies about the risks and benefits of marijuana. Now that it is legal in several states, it will be easier for researchers to obtain and test it. If enough positive findings are published, the federal government may decide to regulate it the way it does alcohol and tobacco. A future president may also feel favorably toward it and decide to legalize it in order to stimulate the economy and decrease crime. Ultimately, the future of marijuana use in the United States is uncertain, but there is good reason to believe that it may be legalized within the next 10 years.

As marijuana becomes more socially acceptable in the United States, the push for legalization becomes stronger.

Notes

Introduction: Marijuana: Here to Stay

1. NORML.org, "States That Have Decriminalized." norml.org/aboutmarijuana/item/states-that-have-decriminalized.

Chapter One: The History of Marijuana

2. Quoted in Edward M. Brecher, *Licit and Illicit Drugs*. Mount Vernon, NY: Consumers Union, 1972, p. 298.
3. Drug Enforcement Administration, "Drug Scheduling." www.dea.gov/druginfo/ds.shtml.
4. Quoted in Brecher, *Licit and Illicit Drugs*, p. 408.
5. Quoted in Larry Sloman, *Reefer Madness: A History of Marijuana*. New York, NY: St. Martin's Griffin, 1998, p. 48.
6. Quoted in Brecher, *Licit and Illicit Drugs*, p. 411.
7. Dan Wakefield, *New York in the Fifties*. Boston, MA: Houghton Mifflin, 1992, p. 177.
8. Wakefield, *New York in the Fifties*, p. 177.
9. Andrew Peyton Thomas, "Mea Culpas on Marijuana," *American Enterprise*, May/June 1997. www.taemag.com/issues/articleid.16187/article_detail.asp.
10. Quoted in the *New York Times*, "Bethel Pilgrims Smoke 'Grass' and Some Take LSD to 'Groove,'" August 18, 1969, p. 25.
11. Quoted in the *New York Times*, "Bethel Pilgrims Smoke 'Grass' and Some Take LSD to 'Groove,'" p. 25.
12. Kristy Graver, "Tela Ropa Lives! Writer Who Spent Her Teen Years at Local Head Shop Laments Its Passing," *Pittsburgh Post-Gazette*, May 19, 2004, p. C-2.

Chapter Two: The Physical and Mental Effects of Marijuana

13. Joe L., interview by author. July 8, 2016.
14. Marla Paul, "Casual Marijuana Use Linked to Brain Abnormalities," Northwestern, April 16, 2014. www.northwestern.edu/newscenter/stories/2014/04/casual-marijuana-use-linked-to-brain-abnormalities-in-students.html.

15. Joseph M. Rey, Andres Martin, and Peter Krabman, "Is the Party Over? Cannabis and Juvenile Psychiatric Disorder: The Past 10 Years," *Journal of the American Academy of Child and Adolescent Psychiatry*, October 2004, p. 20

16. National Institute on Drug Abuse (NIDA), "Is Marijuana Addictive?" March 2016. www.drugabuse.gov/publications/research-reports/marijuana/marijuana-addictive.

17. Christopher, interview by author. July 7, 2016.

18. National Highway Traffic Safety Administration, "Drugs and Human Performance Fact Sheets: Cannabis/Marijuana." www.nhtsa.dot.gov/people/injury/research/job185drugs/cannabis.htm.

19. National Highway Traffic Safety Administration, "Drugs and Human Performance Fact Sheets."

20. Quoted in Theresa D. McClellan, "Teen Gets Jail Time for Fatal Crash," *Grand Rapids Press*, March 22, 2006. www.mlive.com/news/grpress/index.ssf?/base/news-28/11430424515160.xml&coll=6.

21. Quoted in NPR.org, "Transcript of NPR's Interview with Armstrong Biographer Laurence Bergreen," 1997. www.npr.org/programs/specials/hotter/interview.html.

22. Peter A. Fried, "Behavioral Outcomes in Preschool and School-Age Children Exposed to Marijuana: A Review and Speculative Interpretation," National Institutes of Health, p. 242. www.nida.nih.gov/pdf/monographs/monograph164/242-260_Fried.pdf.

23. Joe L., interview by author. July 8, 2016.

24. National Institute on Drug Abuse (NIDA), "Is Marijuana a Gateway Drug?" March 2016. www.drugabuse.gov/publications/research-reports/marijuana/marijuana-gateway-drug.

Chapter Three: Modern Marijuana Use

25. National Drug Intelligence Center, "National Drug Threat Assessment 2005: Marijuana." www.usdoj.gov/ndic/pubs11/12620/marijuana.htm.

26. Quoted in BBC News, "Sir Paul Reveals Beatles Drug Use," June 4, 2004. news.bbc.co.uk/1/hi/entertainment/music/3769511.stm.

27. Quoted in BBC News, "Sir Paul Reveals Beatles Drug Use."

28. Quoted in Vanessa Grigoriadis, "The Most Stoned Kids on the Most Stoned Day on the Most Stoned Campus on Earth," *Rolling Stone*, September 16, 2004, p. 70.

29. Quoted in Sloman, *Reefer Madness*, p. 262.

Chapter Four: Marijuana as Medicine

30. Ryan G., e-mail interview by author. July 7, 2016.

31. Quoted in Brian Preston, *Pot Planet: Adventures in Global Marijuana Culture*. New York, NY: Grove, 2002, p. 255.

32. Quoted in Preston, *Pot Planet*, p. 257.

33. Quoted in Preston, *Pot Planet*, p. 255.

34. Roni Jacobson, "Medical Marijuana: How the Evidence Stacks Up," *Scientific American*, April 22, 2014. www.scientificamerican.com/article/medical-marijuana-how-the-evidence-stacks-up/.

35. Jacobson, "Medical Marijuana: How the Evidence Stacks Up."

36. Quoted in *Consumer Reports*, "Marijuana as Medicine," May 1997. www.medmjscience.org/Pages/history/consumer-reports.html.

37. Quoted in *Consumer Reports*, "Marijuana as Medicine."

38. Ryan G., e-mail interview by author. July 7, 2016.

39. Quoted in *Consumer Reports*, "Marijuana as Medicine."

40. Bailey Rahn, "6 Smoke-Free Ways to Consume Cannabis," Leafly. www.leafly.com/news/health/6-smoke-free-ways-to-consume-cannabis.

41. Quoted in Stephen Henderson, "Court Loss for Medical Marijuana," *Philadelphia Inquirer*, June 7, 2005, p. A-1.

42. Quoted in Erica Werner, "Medical Marijuana Advocates Implore Congress for Reform," Associated Press, *San Jose (CA) Mercury News*, May 4, 2005. www.mercurynews.com/mld/mercurynews/news/local/states/california/northern_california/11564531.htm.

43. New York State Medical Marijuana Program, "Information for Patients," June 2016. www.health.ny.gov/regulations/medical_marijuana/patients/.

44. Ryan G., e-mail interview by author. July 7, 2016.

Chapter Five: The Battle for Legalization

45. R. Keith Stroup, testimony before the U.S. House Subcommittee on Criminal Justice, Drug Policy and Human Resources, Committee on Government Reform, July 13, 1999.

46. Seth Motel, "6 Facts about Marijuana," Pew Research Center, April 14, 2015. www.pewresearch.org/fact-tank/2015/04/14/6-facts-about-marijuana/.

47. "Marijuana May Be Contaminated with Mold, Mildew," CBS News, December 2, 2013. www.cbsnews.com/news/marijuana-contaminated-with-mold-mildew/.

48. Kelly Phillips Erb, "On 4/20, It's High Time to Think About Taxes, Revenues & Marijuana." *Forbes*, April 20, 2016. www.forbes.com/sites/kellyphillipserb/2016/04/20/on-420-its-high-time-to-think-about-taxes-revenues-marijuana/#7fede8c37647.

49. Quoted in National Organization for the Reform of Marijuana Laws, "European Drug Policy," 2002. www.norml.org/index.cfm?Group_ID=4415#europe.

50. Preston, *Pot Planet*, p. 160.

51. Rick Steves, "Amsterdam's Evolving Relationship with Weed," *The Huffington Post*, August 1, 2012. www.huffingtonpost.com/rick-steves/the-latest-on-marijuana-l_b_1724763.html.

52. Quoted in Brad Turner, "Pot Activists Gather for Annual 420 Event," *Longmont Daily Times-Call*, April 21, 2005. www.longmontfyi.com/Local-Story.asp?id=1382.

The American Civil Liberties Union (ACLU)
125 Broad Street
18th Floor
New York, NY 10004
(212) 549-2500
www.aclu.org
The ACLU is committed to combating injustice and ensuring that
individuals are aware of the rights they have in legal situations. Students who feel they been discriminated against in a possession charge
can contact this organization to learn what options they have.

Drug Enforcement Administration (DEA)
8701 Morrissette Drive
Springfield, VA 22301
(202) 307-1000
www.dea.gov
The U.S. Department of Justice's chief antidrug law enforcement
agency is charged with investigating the illegal narcotics trade in the
United States and helping local police agencies with their antidrug
efforts. The DEA's website includes many reports on efforts by the
agency to break up marijuana rings.

National Institute on Drug Abuse (NIDA)
6001 Executive Blvd.
Rm. 5213
Bethesda, MD 20892-9561
(301) 443-1124
www.drugabuse.gov
Part of the National Institutes of Health, the NIDA's mission is to
help finance scientific research projects that study addiction trends
and treatment of chronic drug users. The NIDA's report, *Marijuana
Abuse*, can be downloaded from its website.

National Organization for the Reform of Marijuana Laws (NORML)
1100 H St. NW
Suite 830
Washington, DC 20005
(202) 483-5500
www.norml.org
NORML's website contains news, position papers, statistics, and reports on marijuana use in America. Students can find a state-by-state breakdown of marijuana laws and the legal penalties faced
by offenders.

Substance Abuse and Mental Health Services Administration (SAMHSA)
5600 Fishers Lane
Rockville, MD 20857
1-800-622-4357
www.samhsa.gov
Heavy marijuana users who feel that they are addicted and need help quitting can contact SAMHSA for information on addiction resources. The toll-free helpline is confidential and provides information in both English and Spanish.

For Further Reading

Books

Allen, John. *Thinking Critically: Legalizing Marijuana*. San Diego, CA: ReferencePoint Press, 2016.
> This book presents the pros and cons of legalization for both medical and recreational use. It includes the most up-to-date information about this issue thus far.

Aronoff, Marc. *One Toke: A Survival Guide for Teens*. Lenox, MA: PorterHouse Publications, 2014.
> With weed's growing popularity and acceptance, it is extremely likely that most students will encounter it at least once, and some will try it when offered. This book discusses the reasons to say no as well as ways to stay safe and healthy if the choice is made to smoke.

Brezina, Corona. *Alcohol and Drug Offenses: Your Legal Rights*. New York, NY: Rosen Publishing, 2015.
> Young people are disproportionately targeted by the police for possession, and a person can be charged with a crime for simply being around someone who is caught with marijuana, even if no one is using it at the time. It is important to know how to avoid situations that could have legal consequences, as well as how to deal with any charges that may be brought.

Goldstein, Margaret J. *Legalizing Marijuana: Promises and Pitfalls*. Minneapolis, MN: Twenty-First Century Books, 2016.
> Margaret Goldstein examines legalization efforts not just in the United States, but around the world. She discusses the progress the movement has made as well as the problems with the policies that are currently in place.

Karson, Jill, and Bonnie Szumski. *Thinking Critically: Medical Marijuana*. San Diego, CA: ReferencePoint Press, 2014.
> This book focuses specifically on the pros and cons of legalizing marijuana for medical purposes only. It includes facts and anecdotes about whether or not marijuana is an effective medicine.

Websites

Criminal Defense Lawyer
www.criminaldefenselawyer.com
> Marijuana laws vary from state to state and are often extremely confusing. This site breaks down the laws regarding driving under the influence, marijuana possession and sale penalties, and medical marijuana laws in an easy-to-understand format.

Live Science
www.livescience.com
> Searching for "marijuana" on this site provides many well-researched articles about this issue, including "Is Medical Marijuana Replacing Other Prescription Drugs?" and "Why Does Synthetic Marijuana Make People Act Like Zombies?"

NIDA for Teens
teens.drugabuse.gov
> This site gives more information about different types of drugs, including marijuana. There are informative videos and a quiz students can take to test their drug IQ.

PolitiFact
www.politifact.com
> Politicians and media outlets make many statements that are not always backed up with facts, inclduing statements about drug use and abuse. PolitiFact researches these statements to determine whether they are false, partially true, or true. Many statements about marijuana made in the news can be verified here.

Snopes
www.snopes.com
> While PolitiFact focuses mainly on statements made by politicians, Snopes is a resource that can be used to fact-check urban legends spread through Facebook posts, other forms of social media, and word of mouth. Most stories seen online or heard from friends about marijuana curing cancer, being added to restaurant menus, or being discovered in outer space can be verified here.

Index

Picture Credits

Anna Collins lives in Buffalo, New York, with her dog, Fitzgerald, and her husband, Jason, whom she met on a road trip across the United States. She loves coffee and refuses to write without having a full pot ready.